LOTTO, LONG-DROPS & LOLLY SCRAMBLES

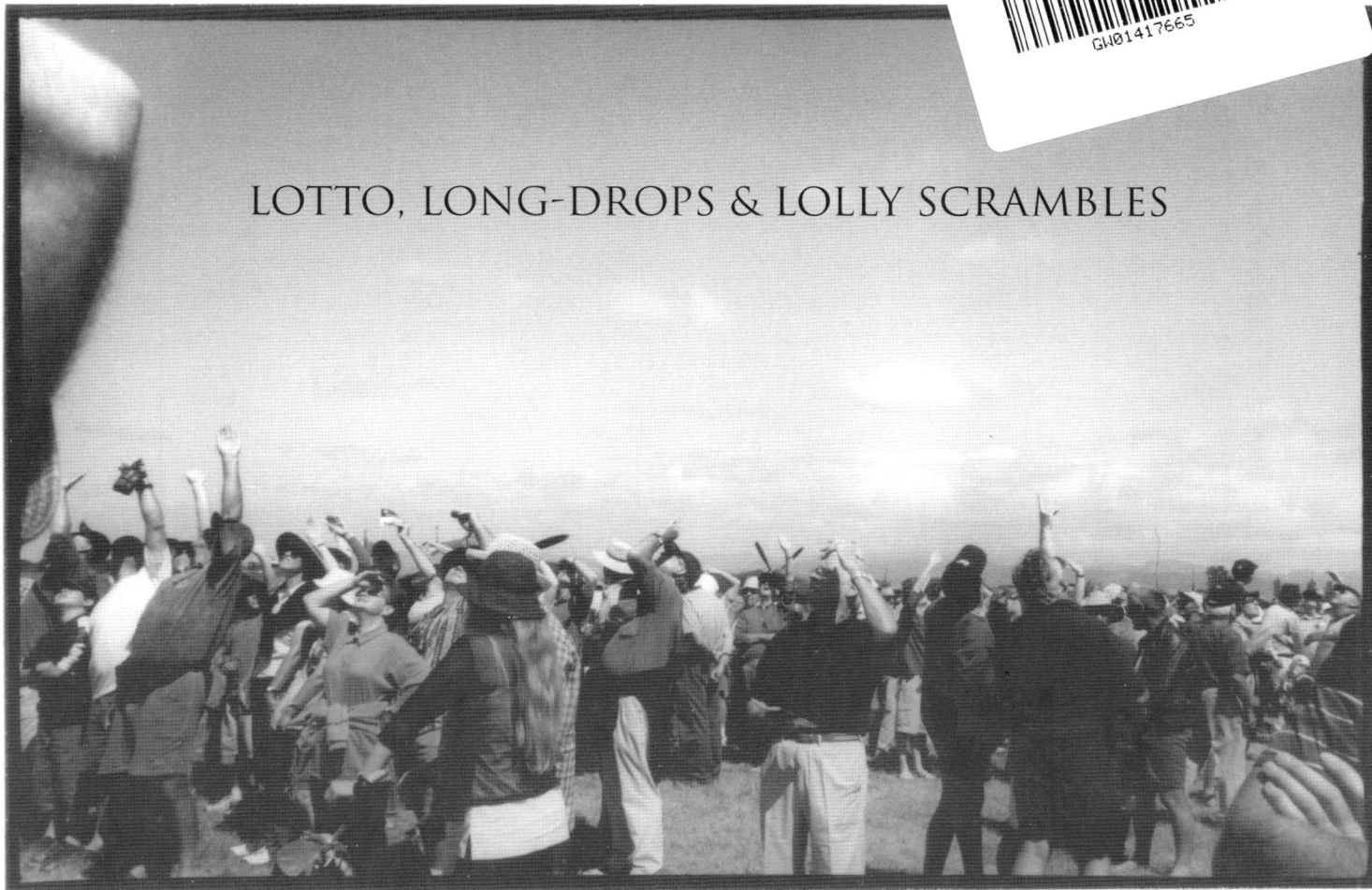

LOTTO, LONG-DROPS & LOLLY SCRAMBLES

THE EXTRA-ORDINARY ANTHROPOLOGY OF MIDDLE NEW ZEALAND

PETER HOWLAND

PHOTOGRAPHS BY LUCINDA BIRCH

STEELE ROBERTS
AOTEAROA NEW ZEALAND

to Karen — the love is unrelenting

Ah, that little asphalt road, so haunted by bitter memories.
We shouldn't overlook the most insignificant spots on earth.
For who knows how much secret grief and joy they may hide.
~ *Zhang Jie*

National Library of New Zealand Cataloguing-in-Publication Data

Howland, Peter, 1961-
Lotto, long-drops and lolly scrambles : the extra-ordinary anthropology
of middle New Zealand / Peter Howland ; photographs by Lucinda Birch.
Includes index.
ISBN 1-877228-74-5

1. Middle class—New Zealand. 2. National characteristics, New Zealand.
3. New Zealand—Social life and customs. I. Birch, Lucinda. II. Title.
305.550993—dc 21

PUBLISHED BY STEELE ROBERTS LTD
BOX 9321 WELLINGTON · AOTEAROA NEW ZEALAND
PHONE (04) 499 0044 · FAX (04) 499 0056
info@SteeleRoberts.co.nz · www.SteeleRoberts.co.nz

CONTENTS

THE COMING OF ANTHROPOLOGY IN MIDDLE NEW ZEALAND ... HOLD ON TO YOUR MOBILES!

ANTHROPOLOGY IS OFTEN imagined to be intrepid research among exotic indigenous cultures. Romantic visions abound of the lone white anthropologist who boldly ventures into the darkest heartlands of tribal society, armed only with a notebook and a firm resolve to understand the fierce-looking natives. More perversely, anthropologists are sometimes thought of as voyeurs *extraordinaire*, revelling in the weirdness of exotic peoples and celebrating diverse practices ranging from infanticide to necrophilia. Gossip abounds of anthropologists with private caches of stone age auto-erotica who undergo ritualised buggery or who keep meticulous 'archaeological' records of their sexual conquests of postgraduate researchers by tagging (i.e. recording event specifics) the relevant undergarments and depositing them in close-to-hand filing cabinets. When anthropologists do venture into Western societies it is mostly on the margins — among bug-eyed drug-takers, the sexually acrobatic or gender-indeterminate. Even within the chummy halls of academia anthropologists are treated with suspicion and caution.

So . . . welcome to my world.

I must immediately state that I do not drive a Toyota, nor am I a fan of country singer Jim Reeves or his Kiwi imitators. I am, however, vitally interested in whether *you* drive a Toyota, have lustful thoughts about John Hore Grenell or even simply watch TV ads. This is because I too, for my sins, am an anthropologist. Well, actually I am the father of two, the lover of one, an enthusiastic but woefully ignorant gardener, a builder of polysemic (i.e. multiple meaning) fences, a lover of fine wine and good food, a fan of Peter Greenaway movies, an admirer of good rugby played by anyone — even the Aussies, a resident of Wellington and the South Wairarapa, a former *Truth* journalist, a homestay operator, a practising atheistic Catholic, and an anthropologist. But definitely not the type who endures bathing in streams, primitive sleeping arrangements and a distinct lack of pinot noir to dissect the cultures of the 'dark-skinned natives' or 'one-legged trans-sexuals.' Rather I am the type who is interested — with an element of analytical voyeurism, I admit — in the people who live, love and die around me. This book, then, is partly a contemplation of my world, and quite possibly of yours too.

Lotto, Long-drops & Lolly scrambles has modest aims — foremost to break even, although a small profit to enable dinner at the Boulcott Street Bistro would be nice. The second is to introduce people to the wonder-full world of anthropological observation, analysis and theory. This can be a potentially life-altering experience. I have known people who, after immersing themselves in such study, have left their partners, renounced their religions and even changed sexual orientation. But all this pales in comparison to one really committed anthropologist who underwent ritual sub-incision — splitting the penis along the length of the urethra — as part of his research into the masculine sexuality of an Aboriginal group in Australia (ironically he was gay and these particular people did not recognise homosexuality). My aim is not necessarily to alter your lives to such a drastic extent, but simply to encourage anthropological ways of thinking about our social and cultural existence. Which leads to my third aim, which is to apply this thinking to the analysis of middle New Zealand. Some of my essays deal with the everyday in New Zealand culture — like toilets, symbols and rituals. Others deal more directly with the Kiwi middle classes in all their thoroughly-scrubbed glory, and look at core ideals and values.

A note of caution, though: anthropology is an unashamedly (some allege conveniently) interpretive discipline. This means that individual anthropologists analyse social and cultural circumstances in ways shaped by their age, gender, sexual preference, domestic circumstances (e.g. with or without children), class background, political viewpoint or theoretical bias. Hence my previous and enthusiastic statement of self. As an academic trained in post-modern sensibilities, I am positioning myself so that you, the reader, can interpret my interpretations, and if we ever get together I can then interpret your interpretations and on we go — generally there is no end to this type of anthro-madness. Any insights I offer on middle New Zealand are based, in part, on my direct research on such things as Lotto, Pakeha ethnicity, and on wine, tourism and class identity in Martinborough, South Wairarapa.

I have always been a curious observer of our culture. I grew up in a working class family in 1960s Upper Hutt and my parents, like many, had hopes that their children would one day transcend their class of birth. Education was seen as the best way to escape the backbreaking ethos of the working class. After a few stumbles, bumbles and deliberate wrong turns I eventually graduated from Wellington Polytechnic as a journalist — a pen-pusher, wordsmith, meaning-maker, truth-twister — and as a nascent member of the middle classes. Then, to cut a long story short, I went to varsity, trained as an anthropologist, fell in love with jazz and enrolled my children in private schools. Change complete.

> *… this pales in comparison to one really committed anthropologist who underwent ritual sub-incision — splitting the penis along the length of the urethra*

A large part of the inspiration for *Lotto, Long-drops & Lolly scrambles* actually came from my experiences lecturing students at Wellington Polytechnic. My job was to teach introductory anthropology to students of nursing, midwifery, dental therapy and environmental health. All were learning hands-on skills, and anthropology must have seemed a waste of their precious time. The challenge was to make the concepts and analysis applicable to their everyday lives — personal and professional. It was a challenge the students took up with gusto, making it clear when I had hit or missed the mark — especially the midwifery students who were always a few steps ahead of me.

Of all the social disciplines, anthropology is the widest-ranging. It involves everything from linguistics, primate studies, criminal forensics, archaeology and the ethnographic study of small-scale societies, through to analysis of world systems and historical processes. Some anthropologists even devote them-selves to observing and analysing rubbish dumps. I practise social and cultural anthropology, so I am interested in the meanings, values, knowledge, actions and interactions of groups of people. The way I collect data, via participant observation, differs from other social sciences. It means I observe and take part in the lives of the people I study. This may involve living in a tribal society for several years, or in my case, playing Lotto and working on a vineyard. I simply couldn't face fieldwork that did not include cool beer in the fridge and the opportunity to bet on the Melbourne Cup.

In this book I use cross-cultural and historical analysis to show the degree to which culture (and most social life) is made by humans. You're not born with your culture — it doesn't exist in your blood, nor is it fixed or bound by time, just waiting for you to possess or rediscover it. All of us learn our culture and then creatively reproduce it on a daily basis. As long as we draw breath we never stop making and remaking culture. In many societies this may continue long after mortal death, as individuals move on to inhabit the active realms of ancestors and spirits. More importantly, as all cultures are human creations they can differ radically between peoples separated by time, place, history, environment, technology and ideas.

This raises the question of what culture actually is. At one level it's a model to describe and analyse what people say and do to each other. But culture is also what people believe it to be. So Kiwi culture, New Zealand culture, Maori culture, wine culture, female culture and rap culture are all forms of what can be thought of as culture. For me, culture specifically resides in individuals who can *meaningfully* interact. If people have this capacity then what they share in terms of knowledge, meaning and actions is culture. And although cultures come and go — the Incas, the ancient Greeks — no living person has ever been without culture.

The boundaries of any culture are fuzzy and almost impossible to plot exactly as the behaviour of individuals is notoriously adaptable and constantly changing. People living in the same place and time may share different aspects of a culture. My father and I share a lot of culture including language, basic categories of understanding (e.g. what constitutes a tree) and behaviour (e.g. gambling on horses). But because of our different experiences and knowledge garnered over time, we also have aspects of cultural difference. I can have no deep understanding of what it was like for him to live in 1940s New Zealand, other than by listening to the stories he tells or reading books and watching films about this era. Likewise, my father's understanding of my anthropological experience is limited to the tales I choose to spin. So are we from the same culture? Hell yes! This is because we can meaningfully interact, even if we don't always agree with or fully comprehend each other. Confused? Well, join the club. Anthropologists are constantly arguing over what does or does not constitute culture, society, the individual and a host of other things — actually, anthropologists are always arguing, period.

Another word of warning. Like many anthropologists I use the term *culture* to refer to the entirety of human existence — all social acts, meanings, knowledge, economics, politics, symbols, you name it. But I also use the term to refer specifically to the meanings, concepts, symbols and values of a people — the thinking, feeling and expressive components of their existence — as opposed to their social life, which may be thought of as their actions and interactions. Hopefully this difference will be obvious in the context.

In this book I have mostly avoided using Maori examples for cross-cultural analysis. I have found that many of us — Pakeha, Maori and others — are far more willing to think about the arbitrariness or constructed nature of our lived culture when comparing it with exotic, faraway others. But I am also making the point that the culture of many Maori includes most if not all of the topics I discuss, such as using ATMs, playing Lotto or planting white crosses on the roadside. In everyday New Zealand the potent mix of things specifically Maori, Pakeha, or generally Kiwi shows how cultures all over the world are increasingly universal, distinctive and interlinked all at once. The logic of transnationalism compels us to simultaneously combine and differentiate cultures … a blend of the familiar and the exotic which makes fertile ground for the tourism industry.

My interest in the anthropology of middle New Zealand does not stem from patriotism, national pride or class and ethnic loyalties. In fact I dislike most collectivities and have long thought of myself as an individual who would rather exist without citizenship, ethnicity, class or any other grouping that has a part in economic, political and social inequity. In other words I am a disaffected white guy (another positioning statement) who lives a fairly comfortable life, but would like champagne on tap. It is the affluence of most academics, intellectuals and other social commentators that enables them to analyse, pontificate and criticise. Without some disposable coin most would be hard-pressed simply to keep body and soul together, let alone to trawl the darker recesses of their minds. So while I may be a disaffected middle-class white guy, I recognise my privilege — I don't just want the champagne for myself, I'd like everyone to be able to guzzle freely.

Naive … possibly, idealistic … for sure, but it's revealing to consider why this ideal state of abundant champagne is consistently thwarted. Much of my analysis is inspired by what social scientists call 'neo-Marxist' theory. This assumes that power is everywhere — in economics, politics, symbolism, interpersonal relations, consumerism, the cultural construction of knowledge, jandal-wearing and so on. It also assumes that power is always expressed inequitably — and no, New Zealand is not and never has been an egalitarian society. Neo-Marxists further assume that all power is inevitably resisted. So whenever I look at a situation I am drawn towards:

■ Highlighting forms of power
■ Detailing the unequal outcomes of power and privilege
■ Finding the power-brokers
■ Identifying those who resist the structures that dominate them — albeit mostly in the hope that they will eventually assume the mantles of power themselves.

I am also interested in the minutiae or humdrum of life because this is where power resides — unseen, unknown and deeply embedded in our daily, mostly unconscious, habits. At one level, anthropology is the study of microcosms in an attempt to comprehend the macrocosm of humanity. I'm fascinated by the daily lives of middle-class Kiwis. Being sandwiched between the bottom and top spectrums of society means that they are equally capable of losing or gaining much cherished power, status and rewards. Yet their overwhelming desire for individual advancement usually means they are the most ardent supporters of hierarchical power structures and merrily subscribe to the inequities of a class system — even though this ultimately denies most of them top-dog status and reward.

When I talk of middle New Zealand I am referring to the middle classes and also to the 'normal' or everyday. Co-incidentally, I am also referring to the geographical middle of New Zealand, namely Wellington and its surrounding districts. The focus of *Lotto, Long-drops & Lolly scrambles* is very much on the generalised experiences of New Zealand's urban middle classes, who are predominantly (but not exclusively) Pakeha or New Zealand European. Many academics will deplore such a stereotypical social category. They will point to the fact that differences in gender, age, sexual orientation, ethnicity, class, urban–rural residence, individual values and so on will result in widely different social and cultural outcomes. Of course they are right. My defence is that one has to start somewhere. Besides, most of us share a culture in New Zealand — at least at the level of language, basic concepts, general understandings and social acts — so we can all potentially relate to the concept of middle New Zealand, even if it does not specifically reflect the particular lives we lead. In this sense, middle New Zealand operates as a model against which any differences can later be compared.

Indeed, the entire idea of social class is hotly contested. Academics, politicians and others constantly disagree on what makes or separates different classes — some even claim that social class has become irrelevant in the current post-modern environment of hyper-individuality. Without going into a convoluted discussion about these disputes, we need only note that most commentators have focused on how employment, wealth, education, class-consciousness and cultural capital (i.e. distinct knowledges, practices, values, etc) create social class. Attachment to a social class can be either unconscious or conscious, and you may ascribe to the core beliefs and practices in the absence or even over-abundance of wealth. The professor of English who watches rugby league, regularly eats meat pies and rides a Norton motorbike; the street-cleaner who writes poetry, sings opera and reads Kant on the weekends; both are potentially cases where class stereotypes do not mesh.

Nevertheless, prosperity enables many people to embrace different class-based ideals (tertiary education, fine wine, etc). So for argument's sake we can assume that most members will be relatively affluent, educated to tertiary level and generally employed in white-collar jobs. Yet many blue-collar workers similarly possess the necessary wealth, learning and social sensibilities to be middle-class.

Working with these assumptions we note that the 2001 New Zealand census revealed that 64% of the labour force were employed in stereotypical middle-class jobs (service and sales, legislators, administrators, managers, professionals, etc), while only 31% were employed in so-called blue-collar work (trade workers, agriculture and fisheries, plant and machine operators/assemblers, etc). The census also revealed that the largest occupational category was service and sales workers (242,508), followed by professionals (239,616), clerks (216,471) and legislators, administrators and managers (216,366). The largest blue-collar category was trade workers (145,296), followed by plant and machine operators/assemblers (144,015) and agriculture and fishery workers (137,484). The single largest job group, by a wide margin, was sales assistants (85,530) — the catalysts of consumerism. General clerks ranked second at 55,311 and paste-up artists came last with only six members. The statistics further revealed that 799,974 — approximately 28% — of the population 15 years and over hold a post-school qualification, bachelor degree or higher. With these figures in mind, it appears safe to declare that New Zealand is dominated by the middle class — God bless them.

So what characterises New Zealand's middle classes? Although differentiated by age, gender, ethnicity, employment, education and wealth, they nevertheless share an ethos that idealises individuality. The unfettered and vibrant expression of individualism is considered by many to be the ultimate goal of a healthy capitalist society, democracy and meritocracy (a society where advancement is based on individual merit). They also share the idea that education and wealth are the primary ways a person's individuality can be creatively nurtured and expressed. A widespread consensus exists that the better your education, the greater the possibility of acquiring hefty wads of cash and the more likely you are to be able to realise your true self. Hence many parents break their bank balances to ensure their children get a vocationally directed education to tertiary level, while they themselves regularly upskill, and spend weekends curled up on the couch with self-improvement books.

One area where New Zealand's middle classes diverge is on the relative merit they attach to schooling or lucre as the ideal method for asserting their individuality. Those who complete commerce degrees may express their ideal selves by driving fast cars, riding jetskis and indulging in expensive stimulants — stiff drinks, sensuous lovers, cigars and salary increments. Others, especially those who trained in the humanities and arts, will place far greater stock on study and its capacity to instil a con-templative love of classical music, theatre, art and well-written books (ideally penned by themselves). Some of this ilk are drawn to other forms of knowledge — from spiritual greenism to Tantric sex — in the very middle-class belief that if everyone were to fully realise their true selves, it would ultimately lead to the salvation of all peoples, the environment and the universe. Those who have studied law fit somewhere in between. They acquire the culture of skiing Mount Hutt and James K Baxter's poetry, together with a clearly exalted sense of self-worth that is reflected in charge-out rates of 15-minute units.

What probably sets New Zealand's middle classes apart from those elsewhere is that many of us are still self-effacing about our social privilege. We often save our conspicuous displays of wealth and privilege for appropriate and compartmentalised occasions. We mostly congregate at black-tie wine clubs, high-class restaurants, the opera or other élite events far from the gaze of the great unwashed. Despite this, a new breed of MBAs are likely to display their class by wearing Gucci to work and eating expensive, account-paid lunches at sidewalk cafés. Yet many Kiwis still cling to the fantasy of an egalitarian society. They spurn acts of conspicuous consumption and are ever-prepared to roll up their sleeves and lend a helping hand to the less fortunate — though this does not necessarily reflect a heartfelt commitment to the ideals of social altruism. In the first place, an empathy with the misfortune of others is a matter of good form, but there is also an element of there-but-for-the-kindness-of-Amex-go-I. Furthermore, New Zealand is a small country and anyone who falls from grace — a regular occurrence given the fickle nature of competitive market capitalism — is likely to find that every sordid detail of their demise is quickly communicated along the country's ever-active bush telegraphs. It certainly pays to have friends on all sides of the roundabout of outrageous fortune.

Hopefully this book will also make some friends. There are eleven essays, this being an anthro-dozen — always one less than expected, hence the compulsion to keep searching for answers. All include suggested readings you might like to pursue in the future. The essays are written for a non-specialist but literate audience, such as Kim Hill's groupies.

Part of my inspiration comes from an eminent American anthropologist who once called on his colleagues "to explore the dialogic modalities inherent in the ethnographic enterprise." My initial response was — *huh*? Then I realised he was rallying anthropologists to find innovative ways of including their objects of study — their human subjects — in the process of *doing* anthropology, from co-authoring books to attending academic conferences. Then I thought about how your average Kiwi on a No. 9 bus would respond to having their dialogic modalities explored by an inquisitive ethnographer. Probably by punching the researcher in the nose or accusing them of making an indecent proposal. So I turned to the work of Margaret Visser, whose books *The Way We Are* and *The Rituals of Dinner* brilliantly apply basic anthropological insight to Canadian culture in a way that is accessible to the average newspaper reader. From here I decided that the main focus of *Lotto, Long-drops & Lolly scrambles* would be a more comprehensive look at middle New Zealand, written for the average middle-class reader.

bollocks to that — they should have never allowed me out of my cage, let alone fed me bananas!

ACKNOWLEDGEMENTS

The essays have been complemented by the quirky photos of Lucinda Birch. When I first saw Lucinda's work I was captivated by her ability to catch the outlandish in the seemingly ordinary. I was greatly pleased that once I had explained the concept of the book Lucinda responded to the challenge. This book would not have been possible without the unrelenting support, constructive criticism and timely advice of Karen, my lover and partner in anthropological transgressions. I also thank my children, Estlin and Corinna, who are a constant source of encouragement, humour and insight. My good friend Ian Day, equally a lover of good food, art and scholarship, deserves a special thanks. He read and critically commented on every essay, constantly drawing my attention to gaps in my knowledge of New Zealand society. My PhD supervisor, intellectual mentor and paternal friend, Dr James Urry of the Anthropology Department, Victoria University of Wellington, has also been a resolute source of intellectual sabre-rattling and menace. He will no doubt recognise many of his ideas throughout this book. I would also like to thank all the academics, fellow postgraduates and students I have encountered along the way. All have challenged and enriched my intellectual life. Then there is my publisher, the consummately laconic and astute Roger Steele, and his affable sidekick Henry Feltham, who saw some glimpse of promise in my initial scribblings and gently guided me to do better … and better … and better (those of you who know Roger and Henry will know what I mean). Thanks to Astral Sligo for the index. At this point in an academic book or journal article it is customary, after acknowledging the assistance of various people, to state that despite their best efforts: "All omissions and errors of fact remain my responsibility." Well bollocks to that — they should have never allowed me out of my cage, let alone fed me bananas!

For a substantial entrée, dip into these general anthro-texts:

Carrithers M (1992) *Why humans have cultures: explaining anthropology and social diversity*, Oxford University Press

Harris M (1980) *Culture, people, nature: an introduction to general anthropology*, New York, Harper & Row

Haviland W (1985) *Anthropology*, New York, Holt Rinehart & Winston

Ingold T (ed, 1994) *Companion encyclopedia of anthropology*, London, Routledge

Keesing R (1981) *Cultural Anthropology: A Contemporary Perspective*, New York, Holt Rinehart & Winston

Kottak C (1997) *Anthropology: The Exploration of Human Diversity*, New York, McGraw-Hill

Roseman A & P Rubel (1995) *The Tapestry of Culture: An Introduction to Cultural Anthropology*, New York, McGraw-Hill

Visser M (1991) *The Rituals of Dinner: The Origins, Evolution, Eccentricities, and Meaning of Table Manners*, New York, Grove Weidenfeld

— (1996) *The Way We Are: The Astonishing Anthropology of Everyday Life*, Boston, Faber & Faber

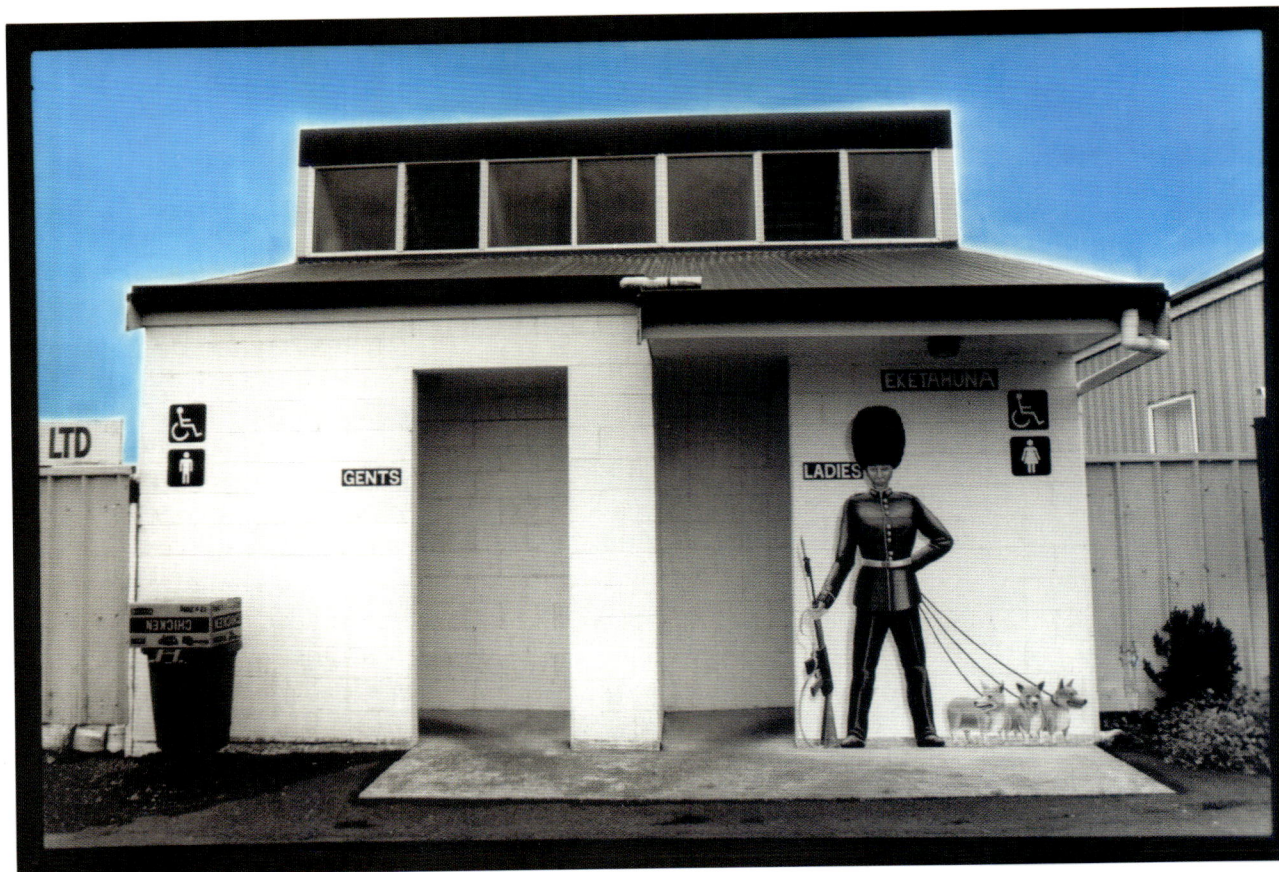

I

LIFE'S A DUNNY ... ANTHROPOLOGICALLY SPEAKING

ANTHROPOLOGISTS, CULTURAL DIFFERENCE & TOILETS

EVERYONE FROM THE QUEEN of England to the hunter-gatherer pygmies of the Andaman Islands — whatever their culture, ethnicity, age, gender, sexuality or social status — defecates and urinates. In many ways the removal of solid and liquid waste from the human body, as an experience common to us all, defines a universal humanity. That is, if your body works according to the natural dictates of biology. If it doesn't then you're about to explode and I recommend you immediately open the nearest can of stewed prunes and grab a spoon.

For many anthropologists, the universality of human waste — like many other natural functions such as menstruation, ejaculation and childbirth — is embedded in, and viewed through, culture. The Hua of Papua New Guinea's highlands hold that a foetus is formed from the coagulation of semen with menstrual blood and that repeated post-conception sex is required to feed the growing foetus. Also, if a pregnant woman has sex with more than one man then all are classified as father to the child. In contrast, the Trobriand Islanders of Melanesia deny that sex between a male and female causes pregnancy — rather, they assert that women are impregnated by ancestors while wading through lagoons. The Trobrianders also believe that frequent post-impregnation sex is advisable as semen is necessary for foetal bone growth and later assists with breast-feeding. In a similar vein, menopause appears to mainly affect women of a certain age in Western societies. Few other cultures recognise or accord significance to this supposedly natural condition. Meanwhile the boffins of Western bio-medicine are about to unleash andropause — or male menopause — on unsuspecting men. Sufferers of this new-found syndrome will clearly be distinguished as men of their time and culture.

Defecation and urination transcend their biological origins and can be thought of as constructs that are categorised, given meaning, named, moralised, valued and socially performed within the frameworks of specific cultures. In other words, individuals from different cultures potentially shit, pee, bleed and climax differently, as do people at different moments of history. How, where and when you go to the toilet — like any cultural event — we can further analyse to reveal specific social, economic and political processes. Anthropologists call this *holism* — in that all beliefs and acts are interconnected and interdependent. Analyse one phenomenon and you're potentially analysing a whole series of cultural and social circumstances.

I first became interested in the anthropology of the toilet when I taught at the Wellington Polytechnic School of Nursing and Midwifery. The school had unisex toilets, which for most of its female students was of little concern. This equilibrium was thrown out of kilter whenever male students were added to the mix. The first few weeks of a new school year were unsettling — especially for the outnumbered males. They could be seen hopping from one foot to another, anxiously peering up

> *Lakalai males, on completing their initiation rites into manhood … did their utmost to pretend they did not have an anus.*

corridors, waiting for the moment when the toilets were free of females before dashing in to their obvious relief. I used this observation to discuss with students how culture influences even natural processes and also how, when confronted by cultural difference, such effects may be startlingly highlighted. What the anxious male students were suffering was a mild form of culture shock. Little in their lives had prepared them for public unisex toilets. What were the meanings and values of a unisex toilet? Aside from the perennial seat-up, seat-down debates, exactly what were the protocols? Did you talk with a member of the opposite sex in the next cubicle? If so, what were appropriate topics of conversation? If a female accidentally dropped her tampon whilst entering a cubicle, was it an act of male chivalry to retrieve it and then on bended knee, return it? The permutations were endless. Until that moment, regular use of adult unisex toilets had not been part of the students' culture and this made these seemingly natural processes fraught with uncertainty and anxiety.

For an even greater sense of culture shock consider the Lakalai of New Britain — an island off Papua New Guinea — who have been described as having a 'sex, shit and shame' complex. Adult Lakalai males publicly asserted that they did not defecate as this was something animals and women did. Although women were not branded as animal-like or sub-human, men basically promoted the belief that they were superhuman and innately superior in being further distanced from the necessities of nature. Lakalai males, on completing their initiation rites into manhood (which involved the social segregation of the sexes), did their utmost to pretend they did not have an anus. If a Lakalai man was caught defecating in the bush by a woman he was so unbearably shamed that he was usually compelled to commit suicide or kill the spying woman before she had the chance to inform others of his disgrace. If the shaming occurred in public — a constant worry for any man afflicted with diarrhoea or chronic flatulence — the man had no choice but to top himself.

Further study revealed that the males actually feared that females were superior due to their capacity to naturally reproduce and nurture the matrilineal clans (i.e. descent groups reckoned through the female line), which control social life among the Lakalai. Also, Lakalai men did not consistently maintain the ruse of non-shitting — their sisters and mothers knew of their pretence and cared for them in times of incontinence. What we learn is that the male mythology was geared towards making themselves appear irresistible to any prospective sexual partners, who had to come from a different matrilineal group. Such women were culturally defined as potential enemies. Lakalai men were therefore concerned that marriageable women consider them to be desirable and superior — hence their claims of non-defecation. The holistic analysis of the Lakalai's attitudes to defecation gives us insight into their cultural creations of the nature-culture divide; gender relations, roles and status; age and adulthood; kinship and other socio-political relationships; sexual attractiveness; shame; social sanctions; and the constructs of space (e.g. public, private, bush).

Maori culture has held similarly elaborate beliefs about latrines. Some ancient Maori believed that human faeces — partly because of its resemblance to sweet potato tubers — was food for the dead. Understandably pre-colonial Maori had a marked aversion to excrement and were shocked to discover that the European settlers fertilised their crops with manure. Maori often built latrines on the edge of cliffs jutting over the sea or on top of steep hills. The area where the faeces fell was called kouka, which roughly translates to the realm of death. A latrine usually consisted of two elaborately carved posts, embedded in the ground and supporting a horizontal beam upon which the user would place their feet to squat. Handgrips were placed in the ground in front of the beam to help with balance and were handy for those forced to 'bear down' to overcome frequent constipation caused by eating fern root. The horizontal beam or paepae marked the boundary between the valued activity of the village and the profane area of excrement deposits. Any individual who had taken part in particularly tapu or sacred activities could return to a state of noa or ordinariness by simply biting part of the latrine structure — usually one of the vertical posts. A similar ritual countered the influence of malevolent atua or spirits, such as those that caused illness or gave a warrior fear on the eve of a battle. Thus when Maori say a person would eat excrement, they mean that he or she would go to any lengths, even the most degrading and negative, to achieve their ends.

For those of us over 50, the long-drop evokes links between effluence and affluence — with septic tanks once being the mark of the upwardly mobile

Shitting and peeing are as much acts of culture as they are acts of nature, and there may be nothing more iconic of the New Zealand (especially Pakeha New Zealand) toilet culture than the long-drop. For many the mere mention of the word long-drop evokes memories of rudimentary tramping huts, baches and campsites; summer flies and sluggish winter wetas; Jeyes Fluid and the potent ferment of decomposing waste; the delayed, satisfying thud of a fresh long-drop … the dreaded plop of an old one. The long-drop also signifies holiday time when workaday rules relax. Unlike the domestic toilet, the door of the holiday long-drop may be left open for a view of the stars — or it simply doesn't exist at all. For the urban sophisticate the long-drop symbolises a boundary between the civilised city and pastoral New Zealand … while for those of us over 50, the long-drop inevitably evokes links between effluence and affluence — with septic tanks once a mark of the upwardly mobile.

There was a time when Kiwi notions of age and gender were reproduced in the long-drop. When a boy reached a certain age he was entrusted to fill in the old long-drop and dig the new one. This enabled a young male — standing as it were on the cusp of manhood — to display the pioneering and civilising prowess of his forefathers. In part, a boy's progress was evaluated by his ability to avoid any form of regression towards a primordial state — by not falling into the old long-drop. It was a woman's lot to follow in the footsteps of the all-conquering male by regularly cleaning the toilet seat and ensuring a steady supply of paper. Even with the eventual rise of sophisticated sewage systems nothing much appears to have changed — most plumbers are still male and well paid, while most women still … enough said. The gradual disappearance of the long-drop from everyday life is directly linked to the rise of the middle classes and the progressive change towards indoor toilets and the now obligatory ensuite attached to the master bedroom. Today the long-drop survives as potent metaphor for the wilderness, for a bygone age of rugged pioneership and as a sign of economic hardship.

That the long-drop is specific to New Zealand culture is highly contestable, with Australia, America, South Africa, Sweden, Finland and many other societies all having their own versions of the bush dunny. It is important not to over-exoticise Kiwi toilet culture, as many of our beliefs and activities are part of general Western culture. For example, eating in the toilet is out of bounds in most Western cultures, which classify human waste as innately polluting. Since 2500 BC and the rise of cities throughout Eurasia with complicated waste drainage systems, urine in the West has increasingly been classified as dirty and harmful. Though toxic if consumed in large enough quantities, urine is actually one of the most sterile naturally occurring liquids. Nevertheless, as a general rule of the West, eating and the toilet don't mix. Our domestic building regulations demand two closeable doors between a toilet and a kitchen to ensure that the contaminants of the bathroom don't spoil the pavlova. Paradoxically, our culturally inspired neurosis about human waste can result in the domestic toilet being the most hygienic room in the house, though whether this applies to student flats is debatable. A recent study in America found that your work station — phone, keyboard, etc — has 400 times the germs of your average home dunny.

How we toilet can also evince differences within a specific culture. As a Kiwi infant it is basically okay to 'go' where and when you please, though nappies are some attempt at physical containment. As we gain language we learn that using the toilet is the mark of being 'a big girl' (i.e. of being culturally competent) and are guided through this process by caregivers. Successes become a cause to celebrate, with parents, siblings, grandparents, extended kin, babysitters and even complete strangers crowding into the bathroom to applaud the young child who stands, bare-bummed, proudly holding up their potty for inspection. When old and senile there may be a partial return to this childlike state, with toileting needing adult nappies and caregivers.

… to ensure that the contaminants of the bathroom don't spoil the pavlova

As a rule-of-bum, as a child gets older its toilet is expected to become more private. Firstly, going to the toilet is increasingly done alone behind closed doors, with youngsters eventually being trusted to thoroughly wash their own hands. This results from our private parts being viewed as sexual paraphernalia, and the differences that are assigned to gender as we get older. At some point it is deemed no longer acceptable for a child to toilet in front of the opposite sex, and a young boy out on the town will cease to accompany his mother into the ladies' room. Instead he is gently encouraged to stand (but hopefully not pee) on his own two feet at the men's urinal. Analysis of these changes can be used to plot how Kiwi children culturally and physically transform into adults as their bodies are demarcated from others according to age, gender, context and social relatedness.

The toiletings of adult men and women are generally kept separate, although this does throw up interesting puzzles. Kiwi men who rarely share their domestic ablutions will paradoxically stand shoulder-to-shoulder with complete strangers at a public urinal, happily engaging in polite banter. When nature calls with some urgency these same men will even resort to urinating in public — usually on a lamppost or down an alley. Similarly, blokes who lock the door of the bathroom at home will share communal showers after a game of rugby. In contrast, most woman are socially prohibited from peeing in public but are quite at ease sharing domestic or public toilets with female friends. This can range from the collusive 'nose powder,' with women congregating in the facilities of restaurants, nightclubs and hotels, through to leaving the door of a domestic toilet open, even sitting on the edge of the bath while a female friend washes herself, to ensure an uninterrupted dialogue. This is not simply a local trait — nightclubs in England now provide 'twobicles' or two-person toilet cubicles specifically designed for multi-tasking (i.e. peeing and chattering) women.

It is also curious to note that most Kiwi males are chronically under-represented in the role of cleaning the domestic toilet, but will spend inordinate time sitting above their own charmless by-products reading the paper. The burden of cleaning toilets, together with the bodily emissions of others (dirty nappies, children's vomit), usually falls on women. Bodily waste is generally thought of as dirty and polluting in our culture and those who deal in dirt are not accorded high social status. The superiority claims of many males are reinforced by making women clean the toilet at home. But why women and not a specific caste of undesirable short men who can easily reach the bottom of the bowl? Female bodily emissions and especially those to do with reproduction (menstrual blood, childbirth fluids, breast milk) are felt by many men to be

These delusions of male control explain why so many men sit on the toilet for hours contemplating one of the triumphs of Western culture — the newspaper

especially dirty and are avoided at all costs. The New Zealand advertising industry is even forbidden to use the colour red to represent menstrual blood, which explains why females in TV-land consistently suffer from the menstrual blues. Such female emissions are also thought of as natural, but not the beneficial, romantic 'natural' so beloved by shampoo advertisers. Rather, it's the kind of natural that is seen as inescapable, irrational and beyond the comforting control of culture. The linking of these beliefs means women exist somewhere between — and are thus designated as mediators of — a dirty, unavoidable nature and a clean, manageable culture, which just happens to be under the ultimate control of men. Kiwi women are therefore culturally condemned to fulfil the 'polluted' roles of domestic caregiver, nurse and toilet cleaner.

Conversely, as the self-proclaimed captains of culture, Kiwi males believe that their bodily emissions are under their direct control. From flatulence to nose-picking, belching to defecating, urinating to ejaculating — many think their bodies function in tune with their direct will and are therefore part of the positive, regulatory influences of culture — which itself results from conscious (hu)man action. Men who can 'handle their piss' are cultural heroes and those who can't are subject to ridicule by having the 'piss taken out of them.' Although such claims of superiority do raise questions about why men miss the bowl so frequently, the prevalence of premature (or at least extremely quick) ejaculation and the perennial issue of involuntary nocturnal emissions. Even as a young schoolboy I made a conscious effort to master the seemingly natural processes of bodily, gaseous emissions so I could successfully partake in lunchtime farting and belching competitions with my peers. These delusions of male control also explain why so many sit on the toilet for hours contemplating one of the triumphs of Western culture — the newspaper. This seemingly inconsequential act boldly proclaims that men consider themselves to be the masters of all domains — nature and culture; shit and print, even though they are closeted in the smallest room in the house.

A word of warning about these broad statements — they are not cast-iron codes, and some people in any given culture will think and act differently. Nevertheless, the seemingly physical and biological processes of going to the toilet are significantly mediated by different cultural beliefs and practices. My analysis of the Kiwi toilet highlights our cultural ideas of age, gender, social relatedness, sexuality, dirt, status, time and space. This is without considering the class connotations of enchanted toilets in chic restaurants and five-star hotels. Nor does my examination ponder the legendary toilet tales of travellers to Asia and beyond. A friend of mine became quite indifferent after only a short time of travelling, to using his right hand for eating and to watching hostel proprietors using their feet — sometimes their whole legs — to clear clogged toilets. When I first considered attending Victoria University I was told by someone that the recreation centre had unisex showers. The prospect of communal, mixed-sex bathing appealed to me as highly civilised. Alas, it was mere rumour and I have long since resigned myself to bathing in less enlightened times. And despite my desire for more progressive ablutions, I still regularly catch myself sitting on the toilet reading the *Dominion Post*. Though never on a Sunday — that's reserved for the *Star-Times*.

Close the door while you contemplate these references:

Chowning A (1989) 'Sex, shit and shame: changing gender relations among the Lakalai,' in M Marshall & J Caughey (eds), *Culture, Kin and Cognition*, American Anthropological Association, Special Publication 25

Chun A (2002) 'Flushing in the future: The supermodern Japanese toilet in a changing domestic culture' *The Journal of Postcolonial Studies*, 5 (1)

Douglas M (1966) *Purity and danger: an analysis of concepts of pollution and taboo*, London, Routledge & Kegan Paul

Hanson, FA & L (1983) *Counterpoint in Maori culture*, London, Routledge & Kegan Paul

Hobbs J & T Couzens (1999) *Pees and Queues: The Complete Loo Companion*, Pinegowrie (South Africa), Spearhead Press

Lawrence W (1960) *Clean and decent: the fascinating history of the bathroom & the water closet, and of sundry habits, fashions & accessories of the toilet, principally in Great Britain, France, & America*, London, Routledge & Kegan Paul

Lambton L (1996) *Temples of convenience and chambers of delight*, New York, St Martin's Press

Van Der Geest S (1998) 'Akan Shit: Getting Rid of Dirt in Ghana' *Anthropology Today*, 14 (3): 8-12

Willems H (1999) *North Island back country dunnies*, Auckland, Halcyon Press

www.sulabhtoiletmuseum.org Website of the Sulabh International Museum of Toilets, New Delhi

II

THE RITUALS OF LIFE:
OUT OF THE SHOWER AND INTO THE LOLLY SCRAMBLE

IDEALS, DINNER PARTIES, RITUALS & SOCIAL CHANGE

The rituals of life have a powerful beat,
Puts a tingle in your fingers and a tingle in your feet. Rituals
in your bedroom, rituals in the street.
Yes, the rituals of life have a powerful beat …

MY APOLOGIES TO FANS of Sammy Davis Jnr, but so plentiful, influential and rich in analytical pickings are the rituals of life that an anthropologist like myself is simply compelled to sing — albeit badly and in print. From everyday rituals such as shaking hands when we greet or buttoning our shirts in the morning, to the momentous and highly formalized rites of passage that mark birth, marriage, death and other equally big changes in an individual's life, all rituals are thick with social instruction, cultural values and often mixed meanings. Whether individual or collective, overtly trivial or saturated with in-your-face sentiment, rituals offer deep insight into the multiple workings of any culture. Besides language — the daily use of which is ruled by convention — rituals are one of the main ways we communicate core concepts and ideals and effect social change. Our entire lives are ritualized from birth to death and beyond. From making love to making dinner. From daubing on eyeliner to painting the house. From washing with soap to watching the soaps. Forget so-called Reality TV, we are all cast as intrepid participants in the daily rituals — the constant folding, unfolding and refolding — of our own lives.

Talk of rituals and we inevitably think of the habitual, apparently unchanging traditions we all perform without much reflection. Think of the many rituals that surround Christmas — the raucous office parties, the brightly decorated tree, the generously stuffed turkey, the inevitable Lotto ticket from the in-laws, the recently unwrapped yet quickly broken but absolutely adored children's toy, the Queen's message, the frantic search among the tide of present wrappings for the TV remote, indigestion, cold turkey or ham sandwiches in the evening, and fridge-cold pavlova for Boxing Day breakfast. While some may momentarily wonder about the origins of kissing under the mistletoe, for most of us it is usually a matter of simply puckering up and getting on with it. Like most of our culture, we simply *do* rituals. We can competently perform most everyday rituals without resorting to deep analysis. We are Zen-like experts and even when confronted by a particularly big-time ritual that is outside our routine there is usually a phalanx of other specialists — from priests to government bureaucrats — on hand to guide us through its complexities and nuances.

Being able to do most rituals without thinking does not mean that we are robotic dolts mechanically reproducing tradition. Rather, most of us are dynamic actors and we invariably change, invent or adapt rituals to reflect the ceaseless changes in our lives. Your role in a ritual may vary over time with your social status. Perhaps you'll think about your changing roles in Christmas gift giving and receiving. As children we tried to convince Santa (or any nearby emissary) that we had been good all year and then excitedly unwrapped our gifts at 5am on Christmas morning. As we became older and the magic surrounding Santa waned we became gift-givers in our own right and took an active part in the conspiracy of Christmas, ensuring the myth lived on for younger generations. As parents we eventually have the prime responsibility for Christmas — surreptitiously buying Santa's presents, dressing up as Santa and so on.

Rituals themselves change over time. In my boyhood, as a practising but woefully unconvinced Catholic, Sunday mass was a time when we papists congratulated ourselves on our especially blessed state to the exclusion of all others — collectively known as heathens, but variously identifiable as Protestants, Anglicans and the damnable rest. Yet in my research into the wine culture of Martinborough I've attended several Christian services, all of which were ecumenical and even praised the followers of Hindu, Jewish, Muslim and other non-Catholic religions. Such all-inclusive celebrations reflect a growing trend towards the break-down of divine boundaries — in places where religious faith is not closely linked to economic, political and other robust forms of secular power as it is in Ireland, Afghanistan and the US.

In many instances specific individuals can be the catalysts of ritual change. The highly energetic but constantly underrated All Black hooker Hika Reid was the prime mover in transforming the All Black haka during the tour of Argentina in 1985. Before this All Black hakas were cumbersome, stilted, almost comical. Rather than displaying the ferocity and awesome physicality of Maori warriors, the All Blacks looked like foot-tied farmers embarrassingly stumbling around the dance floor at the local country hop. Under Reid's expert tutelage the All Blacks eventually mastered the inspiring dynamics of the haka so that it resembled those done by Maori. This reflected a general trend in New Zealand society towards appropriately celebrating and utilising Maori culture. Thanks to Reid's efforts the All Black haka has became a potent weapon in the psychological warfare that surrounds international rugby. As my mentor James Urry is apt to say: "Nothing changes faster than tradition."

Rituals constantly change in form, content and significance as they mirror similar shifts in our lives. But whether rituals are performed unthinkingly and conservatively, or are consciously and purposefully transformed, all have key social and cultural functions. Firstly, they express core ideas and ideals. The simple rituals of dressing in different types of clothing can signify an ensemble of cultural ideas, for instance about context, time, occupation, and gender. Most Kiwis wear street-clothes or civvies to work — with sombre suits reserved for professionals, and overalls or bum-crack shorts for those who work in blue-collar trades. At home most of us revert to casual wear such as jeans or comfortable slacks. As bedtime approaches we are likely to slip into a pair of flannelette pyjamas or something altogether more revealing. Many people — from managers to nurses, labourers to high school students — on their return home feel they must immediately change out of their workaday clothes. For some, their work clothes are physically dirty, or they want to keep them clean for tomorrow. But it is an anthropological truism that *dirt* is simply 'matter out of place,' and in changing attire we create symbolic boundaries between home and work; we are ritually transformed from professional journeymen-and-women to domestic homebodies, and back again the next morning.

How would you react if someone you invited over for a romantic evening, while clambering into bed, refused to remove their Armani suit, Versace socks and Gucci shoes?

This apparel symbolism is not merely aesthetic; the rituals of dressing, undressing and redressing create different values, contexts and social action. To grasp how this works it is sometimes useful to imagine the opposite. How would your colleagues respond if you turned up at work in a silk nightie or in a crumpled bed-weary T-shirt (although you are liable to be arrested for indecent exposure shortly after leaving home). Conversely, how would you react if someone you invited over for a romantic evening, while passionately clambering into the bed-chamber, steadfastly refused to remove their Armani suit, Versace socks and Gucci shoes? You might wisely decide to strike them from your list of potential marriage partners despite their obvious affluence and sartorial splendour. Or try wearing a bikini or speedos to the funeral of a close relative. Unless the deceased was some sort of surfing guru, the chances are your immediate family will publicly disown you long before the eulogies begin.

If this all sounds far-fetched just cast your mind back to the furore that former WINZ supremo, Christine Rankin, caused when she wore long, dangly earrings; short, tight skirts and low-cut blouses. Many commented that she looked more like a Vivian Street slapper, or at best a receptionist in a trucking firm, than a CEO of a major government agency — and proceeded to judge her work ethic and professionalism accordingly. Yet had Ms Rankin worn more conservative suits to work and reserved her personal take on fashion for casual or leisure activities, I believe that most people would have favourably commented on her sense of free-spirited style away from the bureaucratic rigours of institutionalised goodwill. Rankin's folly was in failing to clearly demarcate work and fun — a boundary that is religiously adhered to in New Zealand.

Many rites of passage are similarly rich with the nuances of dressing and associated cultural ideals. In a typical North American wedding the virginal (or at least sufficiently chaste) bride will proudly wear a white wedding dress to display her virtue, although under this gown of honour she may be sporting a sexy garter belt to signify her wild side. At an appropriate moment in the nuptials the bride lifts her gown to reveal the undergarment, which her newly-wed husband then removes — often with his teeth — before throwing it to the attendant bachelors. Later the bride darts away to change out of her bridal dress and into her honeymoon gear before roaring off into the distance with her lecherously grinning hubby in tow.

Such bridal rituals symbolise her change in social roles. Dressing in a white gown signifies that a woman is a suitable candidate as a bride and announces the start of the rite of passage that will transform her from a single to a married woman. As the bride reveals her garter belt we literally and symbolically glimpse her saucier temperament — the side of her that snared a potential husband. Indeed when her husband removes her garter and throws it to the bachelors we symbolically see how he has exclusive dibs on his bride's carnality, and accordingly informs the other males to search elsewhere. Similarly, when the bride ritually throws her bouquet to the anxiously waiting unmarried women, she signifies that she has bloomed into full, monogamous womanhood and is passing the seed of wedlock onto the next in line. After the ceremonies, speeches, eating and dancing, the bride changes back into civvies and symbolically transforms into an everyday, but now very married, woman.

Similar rituals can also be seen when individuals — and especially women — go through the processes of marital conflict, separation and divorce. Many continue to wear their engagement and wedding rings throughout the initial conflict. If the couple then separate, some women move their rings to the opposite right finger. After divorce papers are final they may remove their rings completely. I know one who then stored her rings in a jewellery box. Many months later when she had 'moved on' with her life she sold the rings and used the proceeds to build a deck onto her house, where she now regularly enjoys gin & tonics and the feeling that she has finally come out on top. Others I have known have given their rings to their daughters, who then wear them on their right hands to indicate that they are not married.

Most rites of passage involve three phases. First, *separation* from your current social role, status or situation; second, *liminality* or being betwixt 'n' between; and finally *re-incorporation* into a new social role, status or circumstance. In the liminal phase individuals are encouraged to play with or even subvert widely held ideals and behaviours before committing themselves to the next stage of their lives. This phase of the ritual highlights the value of the 'normal' by pointing out the potential foibles of alternatives. For example, stag parties typically involve lewd public displays thought to be inappropriate in marriage. Friends of the groom may try to get him wildly drunk, tempt him with strippers and leave him tied naked to a lamppost, in a display that at once symbolises the delights and potential pitfalls of bachelorhood. Once married, the groom is expected to engage mostly in sober pursuits that advance the lot of his new wife and family, to be resolutely monogamous, and to be found naked only in the most intimate domestic settings. If the groom can't fulfil these duties of wedlock this liminal phase gives him the perfect opportunity to scarper with a bottle of bourbon tucked under one arm and a stripper under the other. This tests an individual's capability and willingness to take on the responsibilities demanded by their new social role.

Many rituals in our daily lives show similar transformatory functions. One of my students told me how her large extended family would congregate every Sunday to share a meal. Whilst the roast was in the oven her adult brothers would sit around the dining-room table swapping tall stories and rude jokes. Once the roast was cooked and the table set the family's matriarchal grandmother would take her seat at the head of the table and bow to say grace. From this point the ribald talk ceased and throughout the meal everyone observed the protocols of good manners and polite conversation that so many of us were laboriously schooled in once we had graduated from the highchair to the adults' table. On completing their meals each individual family member would ask the elderly matriarch to be excused. Once away from the table many of the adult men would declare "Bloody Christ, thank God that's over" before belching loudly and resuming their bawdy talk in the lounge. Clearly the rituals of setting the dinner table and saying grace transformed the social environment — previously characterized by salacious,

blokish banter — to one of respectful family fellowship, just as the ritual of asking to be excused and clearing away the plates reversed the context.

My first awareness of the everyday rituals of change came when I was working as a sports reporter in Wales. One morning the gas water heater in my flat blew up and I couldn't have a hot shower. Faced with this problem I returned to bed and phoned the editor to inform him I wasn't able to work. Although I was admittedly disillusioned with journalism at the time I have since become increasingly aware of the value of my daybreak ritual. If any part of my morning routine is disrupted or missing I feel agitated and grumpy all day. This may be due to a lack of caffeine, but it is also caused by my inability to ritually distinguish between my domestic and public personae. In other words, I can become trapped in a liminal state — lamentably betwixt 'n' between, neither domestic nor public, neither homebody nor anthropologist.

Rituals also construct social categories, the most basic of which are *insiders* and *outsiders*. Insiders are those allowed to take part in a ritual, who can competently perform its set pieces and who can comprehend (either consciously or seemingly intuitively) its subtle meanings and significance. Outsiders are simply those who don't.

The rituals surrounding the Kiwi middle-class dinner party are a case in point. Knowing when to arrive, what to wear, what type of wine to bring (so you please and don't embarrass your host with your stinginess/largesse), to bring flowers or chocolates for your hostess, how and when to use your multi-course cutlery, that the mid-dinner sorbet is served to cleanse the palate and not as a dessert, and knowing which topics of conversation are considered appropriate and which are not, are all part of the dinner party ritual. Failure to perform competently in any one part quickly marks an individual as an oaf and an outsider.

But this list of ideal dinner party attributes is just that — an ideal. As with any ritual, the actualities of performance may be at odds with the expressed ideals. One of the most salient features of the middle-class dinner party is how certain people will move from a state of refinement (characterized by feigned indifference, or at least suppressed excitement) to one of vital engagement with assembled others, then finally to a state of unashamed abandonment of social grace. Indifference is first shown by arriving fashionably late. This symbolises that the latecomer is a dynamic individual who has myriad competing calls on their precious time. It also recognises that the hosts are similarly charismatic people who have interrupted their busy schedules to arrange the dinner party and are likely to need all the time they can find to prepare it. However, there is usually a marked gender difference. Many males display the greatest degree of fashionable disdain, and females — hosts and guests alike — are left to make the ritual apologies and build the necessary social bridges.

Failure to perform competently in any one part quickly marks an individual as an oaf and an outsider

As the evening progresses the wine flows more freely and everyone loosens up and engages in lively, even intense banter. But as the wine — and later, hard spirits — continue to flow, this to-and-fro may become ever looser and less polite. An individual's restraint may drop alarmingly and table talk can become quite lurid, argumentative, or even abusive. At this point the participants have moved from the initial distinction of hosts and guests to a sort of collective, no-holds-barred domestic intimacy … which will be reversed when the party ends and guests collect their coats before they go. During this time licence is given to express and even play with innermost tensions or unresolved conflicts. This is a reversal of their public personae in which emotions, vulnerability and less-than-ideal are usually hidden behind a veneer of controlled, upbeat professionalism and middle-class detachment.

For some women this liminal phase of the dinner party allows them to confess that they are sexually dissatisfied. Some make derogatory remarks about their male partners' lack of bedroom prowess — often at the very time their men are conversely bragging about their sexual accomplishments to the assembled guests. Others may candidly flirt with the men (or women) present and, in an interesting reversal, those with the least satisfying sex lives (in quantity and quality) often act in the most lascivious manner — removing their knickers or tops and dancing on tables, men's laps — and other such delights. By comparison, some men can become quite aggressive and stroppy as they seek to dominate and deride the achievements of others. Usually men direct hostility towards those they think have slighted them or who need 'to be taken down a peg or two.' This can involve boasting about their cars, incomes, house values and sexual conquests. Sometimes a man's anger will be openly directed at his partner for her alleged shortcomings in the bedroom, around the house, in raising the children or for squandering his hard-earned dosh. Occasionally it's directed at other women, who may have spurned his sexual advances at a previous dinner party. Some readers may think this is little different from the boorish behaviour typical of many males. But the liminal phase of the dinner party compels many men to publicly acknowledge previously hidden vulnerabilities and difficulties — even if they do eventually revert to their usual 'my dick's bigger than yours' posturing.

Such liminality acts as a safety valve — we need to vent the stresses caused by the incessant demands of daily life. But if the dinner party is of the business kind then this release is markedly subdued. On such occasions hosts and guests are expected to be ready on time and to display their professionalism; and table banter is directed towards reaffirming already established roles, rankings and hierarchies. The alpha male (aka 'the boss') may get tipsy, confrontational and sexually forward, but woe betide any other schmuck who engages in the liminal conflict typical of the friendly middle-class soirée. Shortly after they recover from their hangover they can expect an immediate posting to the company's Algerian office, or at least Taihape.

Most rituals actually seek to accentuate the positive by articulating and reaffirming the shared ideals of the participants. Rituals are key instruments of socialisation. Their repetition ensures that 'initiates' learn appropriate cultural ideals; the already initiated are reminded of their ongoing responsibilities. The lolly scramble is a distinctive Kiwi ritual in which children furiously compete to grab lollies thrown into the air. It is a perfect example of this process, although like most rituals it does not simply accentuate the positive. It also affirms and even resolves the tension between the contradictory ideals of egalitarianism and competitive individualism that are the lot of many middle-class New Zealanders.

Lolly scrambles usually follow a standard format. Firstly, they happen at occasions such as Christmas parties, school galas and the opening of shopping malls, and are given special significance. The person in charge, whose role involves throwing fistfuls of lollies towards the hopeful hordes, is usually an authority figure (e.g. a headmaster) or somehow extraordinary (Father Christmas, a live teddy bear). This promotes the idea that any lessons learned through the lolly scramble are similarly important. At some point the children are commanded to gather round. Smaller children are placed near the front; those who are reluctant to take part are urged by parents to have a go. There is a general expectation that the battle for the lollies will be a free-for-all and that an individual's skill, courage and luck will be the main determinants of their success — although older children sometimes form gangs to increase their competitive advantage. Once the children are assembled the person in charge begins throwing lollies into the air. They constantly alter direction to ensure that every child has at least some chance of snaring a fistful of lollies. In doing this they maintain an air of almost whimsical authority and control, to which the children respond with squeals of delight and protest as they are sent scurrying first one way, then another.

Most children compete furiously for the sweets, with older ones usually securing the lion's share through their obvious physical advantages. Smaller children are encouraged by parents and other bystanders to use cunning to offset any disadvantages: "*Watch him Tommy! He's already thrown left, run to the right!*" When the lolly scramble is over children compare their bounties. Successful ones gloat over pocketfuls of sweets, although in doing so they risk a post-scramble mugging. There are always children who are bitterly let down. Some secure only meagre hauls, others fail altogether, and many more are physically and mentally battered during the ferocious competition. At this point the adults again enter the fray. They congratulate the winners and console the losers through a mixture of strategies such as offering advice on how to do better next time, trying to convince disappointed children that their hauls are in fact substantial, and by taking

Children learn to compete using physical size, cunning and even banditry. They learn that some are winners and others are losers

sweets from the more successful children and redistributing them to the less lucky. Adults warmly praise older children who voluntarily share their loot with younger siblings. At the same time the tight-fisted are chided and 'encouraged' to quickly embrace the practice of charity.

Thus the ritual of the lolly scramble encourages adherence to the seemingly at-odds ideals of competitive individualism and social equality. Firstly, children learn to compete using physical size, cunning and even banditry. They learn that some are winners and others are losers, and that hierarchies of differential reward are to be expected and celebrated accordingly. Children also learn to value authority and its power over the destiny of others. While charity is one positive outcome of this control, the lolly-throwers also stand for a darker side of authority as they scatter lollies at whim and without apparent recourse to regulation or appeal. You can often hear young children wishfully imagining what it would be like to be the lolly-thrower, just as on Saturdays you hear daydreams about winning Lotto. Children discover that their personal edge can be sharpened by either co-operating or competing with others — even by mugging them. As the dust settles they receive their final lessons. Firstly, they learn that families should share, and more broadly that they have an onus to ensure that everyone gets some reward for their effort — at least enough to placate the miffed to ensure they take part in future lolly scrambles. This overtly simple ritual at once champions notions of equal opportunity, competitiveness, reward for endeavour and pragmatic egalitarianism — attributes routinely expressed by our major political parties, the Business Roundtable and the many agencies of social welfare. Whether this ritualized resolution of competing ideals spills over into daily life remains highly debatable.

Compare this with the children's game of *piñata* in North America. Piñata is also played during significant occasions, and again adults are ostensibly in control. The children are blindfolded and take turns at trying to smash open the treat-filled piñata, usually made in the shape of a donkey.

In the Kiwi lolly scramble and the American piñata the rituals of so-called child's play are revealed as deeply serious business.

A great deal of luck is required and the task is made harder by adults calling out misleading instructions and constantly moving the piñata. Once it is smashed open all the children rush forward and the struggle for the spilled treats becomes a free-for-all, although the piñata itself is reserved for the winning child. In this ritual children are socialized in the ideals of rugged individualism and self-reliance that underpin the American dream. They learn the difficulties of securing success in a rampant meritocracy (i.e. a society where advancement is based on individual merit). Not only does this require a balance of individual effort and luck, but others, including close kin and friends, will try to derail your efforts. Even when personal success is achieved and recognized — when the piñata is smashed open and its remains reserved for the conqueror — others will still try to rob you of your just rewards. In the Kiwi lolly scramble and the American piñata the rituals of so-called child's play are revealed as deeply serious business.

All rituals involve displays of social and cultural power: the power to determine which rituals will be performed and which ideals, values and acts will be promoted. Rituals are most likely to serve the interests, and assert the legitimacy, of the most powerful people and ideologies in any society. Hence the opening of the New Zealand parliament is conducted with a type of pomp and ceremony not accorded the unemployed when they sign on at WINZ. What is intriguing about many rituals in New Zealand — and especially rites of passage — is that they are mostly negotiated individually rather than collectively. Getting drunk for the first time, earning a driver's licence or losing your virginity are all rituals that mark points at which we change from child to adult.

When and how you pass these milestones is usually a matter of choice — albeit subject to legal limits and, at times, unrelenting peer pressure. Even in adulthood, the transformatory rituals of owning your first car, getting married, buying your first home or having children are individually negotiated. Although recognized as important, our rituals of social transformation are not usually pursued in collective groups. Instead, we live in a culture that at almost every turn ritually affirms the contradictory ideals of individualism that are so highly valued by the middle classes.

The question remains: does our ritual obsession with individuality enable us to lead truly independent lives? On the surface we clearly assert our particular personalities by (ideally) choosing when we will drink our first beer, whether we buy a petrol or diesel car, or by watching our favourite channel on TV. Recent newspaper adverts for TV One promote this ethos by showing a dizzying array of lifestyle choices from basic diff-erences in gender to an inspiring variety of ribbed, lubed and flavoured condoms. They assert that although 650,000 readers had seen the same material, the 210 choices offered meant that millions of differently configured lifestyles were available for anyone to choose from. Thus ensuring that: *"Not one of us chooses the same; Not one of us is the same; Because we are all individual; Here's to television that understands that; Reflects that; Celebrates that; Choose ONE."*

Obviously many people will certainly make the same choices (e.g. male, own a petrol car, wear Y-fronts, watch rugby, drink lager, use ribbed condoms, etc), and the promotions without any hint of self-deprecating irony encourage everyone to watch the ONE channel. But what these adverts fail to recognize is that simply being able to read, comprehend, count, and even desire choice are cultural traits that are widely shared. It's very much a wood-for-the-trees scenario. Rather than highlighting rampant individuality they actually confirm our commonality, our collective culture and society. It is another anthropological truism that no person is ever wholly individual or distinct. We are all created by, reflect and in turn vigorously contribute to the social and cultural milieus in which we are born, live and die. Hence we are all the by-products of each other. From the moments before and during conception, to being gently lowered into the grave, we are ever reliant on others to enable ourselves. And in contemporary societies such as New Zealand — where we are highly specialised in terms of occupation, knowledge, experience and access to resources — we are far more inter-dependent than our hunter-gatherer forbears. None of us can singularly reproduce all the necessities of life. Simply to enjoy a glass of pinot at home we rely on the expertise of builders, glass foundrymen, petrol jockeys, grease monkeys, winemakers, truck-drivers, vintners, plumbers and sewage operators. True, we are all unique from our DNA up, but much of this individuality is neither socially meaningful or influential. That you sneeze at 9.15pm and I sneeze at 9.16; that you prefer gin and I vodka; that you make love with your socks on and I make love to my socks should not blind us to the reality that we and a whole host of others are all sneezing, drinking alcohol and making hanky-panky. At one level we are unique in our biological make-up, even in the specifics of our experience. But we also act in very similar, if not exactly the same ways, that are largely determined by our shared natures, society and culture. If you regard sock-sex as bizarre, we still share an understanding of what making love is and what socks are, even if you wouldn't volunteer to do the laundry. It is impossible for any of us to totally step outside our cultures and forge completely original lives. Everything we do is historically, socially, economically, politically and culturally contingent. It may be new, hip or revolutionary, but it is still created from and based on what we share with others. Therefore, can we genuinely lead lives that contradict or confound those values that are idealised by our middle-class rituals? Are any of us individual and independent enough to choose lives of total sobriety, chastity, humility and subversion of free will? Or are we all condemned to follow the collective fads and fashions of work, shopping malls and nation-state politics?

In an interesting twist it appears that only those most bound by ritual, who are the most sociocentric and who almost compulsively surrender their free will to a collective, actually lead such lives. I am of course referring to monastic, priestly and other religious adherents, many of whom voluntarily forsake the trappings of middle-class individuality to serve a greater good. But then they are equally constrained by a host of other social processes, illusions and ideals. Without rituals to constantly guide, prompt and beguile us, we would be forever cast adrift on tides of uncertainty … such are the rituals of our lives.

Customary references – a ritualized response:

Bell C (1992) *Ritual theory, ritual practice*, New York, Oxford University Press

Davis S Jnr (1968) 'The Rhythm of Life' music by Cy Coleman, lyrics by Dorothy Fields, in *Sweet Charity*, Universal Pictures

Douglas M (1999) *Implicit Meanings, New & Revised*, London, Routledge

— (1966) *Purity and danger: an analysis of concepts of pollution and taboo*, London, Routledge & Kegan Paul

Van Gennep A (1960) *The rites of passage*, London, Routledge & Kegan Paul

Rothenbuhler E (1998) *Ritual Communication: from everyday conversation to mediated ceremony*, Thousand Oaks, Sage Publications

Turner V (ed, 1982) *Celebration: studies in festivity and ritual*, Washington DC, Smithsonian Press

— (1982) *From ritual to theatre: the human seriousness of play*, New York, Performing Arts Journal Publications

Tuzin D (1980) *The Voice of the Tambaran: Truth and Illusion in Ilahita Arapesh Religion*, Berkeley, University of California Press

III

HAIR COMBS, PAVLOVA AND SILVER FERNS: SIGNPOSTS OF KIWI CULTURE

SYMBOLS, KIWIANA, GLOBALISATION & ROMANCE

A ROSE BY ANY OTHER name would not be a diamond. This is perhaps most evident in the whirlwind domains of romance, where roses and diamonds are widely seen as gifts of love. Even so, they are not equal — their value as gifts depends on the context in which they are given and received. Anyone who has courted, consummated or been rejected in the affairs of the heart will instantly know the romantic minefield that these symbols of love can represent. Present your loved one with a dozen roses when she is impatiently expecting a precious stone and you could find yourself sleeping on the sofa. Conversely, a diamond given too early in a courtship may be met with a firm response that the relationship is moving too fast and a cooling-off period is required. In extreme cases this may quickly be followed by a series of unanswered phone calls, accusations of stalking, then a restraining order.

Every day we encounter thousands of symbols, from traffic signals to hairstyles, room ornaments to body piercings, religious icons to sports uniforms. Symbols are literally the vehicles by which cultures communicate. All culture, from language to everyday signs and everything in between, is symbolic on the basis that it is created by humans to allow meaningful interaction between members of a society. And just as romantic feelings are complicated, symbols and what they communicate are also multi-dimensional. Roses and diamonds, aside from being romantic gifts, are also objects of natural beauty. A gift of either symbolises that your feelings are equally natural or authentic and that you think the recipient is similarly attractive. But a rose is an object of fleeting beauty that once plucked quickly wilts and dies, whereas a diamond is a rare object of permanent beauty that is much more valuable. A diamond also symbolises the control over nature that humanity has honed in an effort to realise its optimum beauty.

A rose can therefore signify ardour, whereas a diamond expresses your commitment to sustain the flames of love through good times and bad. Through similar reasoning, a bunch of daisies given in the early days of courtship allows the giver to express — and the recipient to freely choose from — a bouquet of meanings, ranging from friendship to growing sexual desire.

Actor Brad Pitt displayed enough savvy to send white roses to his ex-girlfriend, Gwyneth Paltrow, to congratulate her on winning an Oscar for her performance in *Shakespeare in Love*. If you get an empty photo frame from your lover, your number may be up — they want you out of the picture and for you to appear with someone else.

Often specific to context, symbols communicate a wide array of information that we read, interpret and respond to on a routine basis. We are highly conscious of many of these. Wear a Hurricanes Super-12 rugby shirt to show support for the team; or burn the same shirt to vent disgust with their repeated losses — both actions send a clear message. Moreover, the picture of a water-dewed apple in the window of a fruit merchant indicates that fresh fruit (including apples) is available for purchase. A similar picture in a doctor's surgery can symbolise good health or, in a dentist's waiting room, righteous dental care. Likewise the image of a voluptuous woman seductively holding an apple in garish neon lights on K Road, Auckland or Vivian Street, Wellington, can advertise the wares of a massage parlour through an allusion to the sexually primordial Eve. How you react to these different symbols depends on your personal proclivities, your cultural or social background, and whether you are subject to moral discipline. A truculent school child may secretly eat sweets in defiance of the healthy apple message and her mother's stern warnings, just as the world-weary husband may be attracted by the neon sign in a red-light street — but only when his wife is out of town.

Anthropologists are mainly interested in three types of symbols: *signs*, *metaphors* and *metonyms*. Most of us are probably familiar with the idea that metaphors are types of symbols that link the attributes of one thing to something else. A stylised apple can signify an *iMac* computer with a metaphorical link to the pursuit of knowledge via Isaac Newton's discovery of gravity and the falling apple. Likewise if we read the biblical tale of Eve in the Garden of Eden we know that the apple plucked from the Tree of Knowledge is a metaphor for original sin. A metonym, on the other hand, is a symbol in which a part is used to symbolise the whole. Thus an apple symbolises ENZA (formerly the Apple & Pear Marketing Board); a crown, the Royal Family; a kiwi, the nation-state of New Zealand.

The idea that a sign is a type of symbol is more difficult to get a handle on. A sign is something with a one-to-one relation to an object, event or other phenomenon — the word or a picture of an apple that represents an apple, say. But how could this be symbolic, because after all an apple is an apple? Equally, how could a pavlova, a kiwifruit or a traffic sign saying STOP also be symbols — aren't they exactly what they are? Yet all symbols (signs included), like all cultural categories, meanings and language, are arbitrary. There is no necessary or innate link between a word and that which it purports to represent. Any meaningful correlation is a product of the human imagination and is often culture-specific. Because we react to most signs in habitual and seemingly instinctive ways we are often unaware of their core symbolic nature. A hair comb or a closed door in Kiwi culture are signs so basic that they appear to be natural. Rather than being thought of as some sort of take on reality, they simply appear to be what actually *is* — to be reality itself. But both are symbols, as their purpose and significance are created in our culture. This can be shown by the fact that as young children we had to learn, formally or by imitation, how to correctly use a hair comb and a door. Our first responses to these objects, which may have involved trying to eat them, were natural. Our competent use of these objects — from opening and closing a door to combing our hair in the morning — is learnt and therefore cultural.

As we mature we learn that many other meanings and acts beyond the functional can attach to such objects. Initially we learn that a comb should not be used as a boat to float in the toilet, then we are taught that its standard use is to tidy our hair. As adults we learn that this is ideally done just before a romantic date but we should exclude combing our hair if later immersed in passionate lovemaking. We also quickly learn that a door is used to enter or exit from one space to another. As such, a closed door may symbolise exclusion or inclusion depending which side you are on. Many of us learnt the hard way to knock on our parents' bedroom door before entering early on a Saturday morning — as many therapists will attest. Eventually most children learn that a closed door can mean privacy, indeed by the time they are teenagers many consciously use this symbolism to communicate a loud *Keep Out!* to the rest of the world.

To understand this line of anthropological thinking on signs it may help to imagine someone from a culture without hair combs or doors. How would they read, interpret and respond to these symbols? Most probably, in terms of the nearest thing like it in their own culture. This could range from seeing the door as a wall with a purposeless handhold, to believing that hair combs are magical devices used to repel evil spirits from attacking the head. The urban myths of Pacific Island immigrants to New Zealand in the 1970s, who reputedly lit fires in electric stoves and 'failed' to flush toilets — although usually told in an exaggerated way as racist put-downs — really have their substance in that the functions and values of such everyday utilities were specific to Kiwi culture and by default foreign to the immigrants' culture. The initial and understandable response of some Pacific Island immigrants was to apply their indigenous knowledge to our culture with obvious resulting confusions. What type of cultural blunders might the average Kiwi have committed had circumstances been reversed? Washed their smalls in a ceremonial kava bowl? Exposed themselves as cultural bozos through being unable to correctly fasten a lavalava? The point is that all symbols — including everyday signs — are constructs and are therefore likely to be given meaning and practised in culturally specific ways.

Some symbols have a marked tendency to be culture-specific. In Chinese cultures the colour red symbolises good luck, happiness and dignity. Charms of this colour adorn houses at New Year festivals and at other auspicious times. In contrast, white represents the west and is linked with death, darkness and sunset. Principal mourners and funerary experts are expected to wear white during funeral rituals. During this period red charms are covered in white cloth. In Chinese cultures white also represents Yin, the female principle. The corpse, which represents human flesh in absence of life (i.e. rotting), is thought of as a dangerous coalescence of female forces and hence polluting. Once properly buried, facing towards the east, the deceased's remains can enter the realm of ancestors and obtain purity (i.e. because they will be flesh-free). At this point their bones are Yang, the male principle, and are linked with the renewal of life, light and sunrise. They also become the exclusive responsibility of males, who practise ritual worship to ensure continued favour with their ancestors. In Kiwi culture the colour red symbolises danger (traffic signals), sexual desire (red-light districts) and excitement (red sports cars). Black is the colour of grief (mourning attire) or other equally serious endeavours (business suits, élite rugby uniforms). White may symbolise purity (virginal wedding dresses), hygiene (a white doctor's coat) or cleanliness (a bleached toilet bowl).

Likewise the symbols of Kiwiana — Buzzy Bee, silver fern, Vegemite, Lemon & Paeroa, the kiwi, kiwifruit, pavlova, the tiki, the black singlet — enjoy little currency beyond our culture. Like many markers of identity, Kiwiana is consciously used to express ideals (see Identity essay), a perfect picture of Kiwi culture in which the chaos, conflict and hardships of life are hidden from view. (Actually, the concept can also be applied to this book, as the drafts, redrafts, editorial disputes, initial spelling and grammatical errors are hidden beyond the book's margins.) At a more basic level these symbols of nationalism are natural. They either:

- Occur in nature (the silver fern)
- Are made from natural products (the pavlova)
- Romantically emulate the natural (the Buzzy Bee)
- Relate to the culture of indigenous peoples (the tiki).

Being linked with nature or the natural gives these symbols an aura of innate authenticity and trustworthiness. Symbols that exist solely in nature — the silver fern, the kiwi — and Maori culture denote an even greater sense of distinctiveness in being native to New Zealand. They invoke potent sentiments of rootedness to the land, society and culture of Aotearoa. Often employed for their iconic qualities, they serve to highlight the apparent uniqueness of being Kiwi, never mind that most nation-states reproduce similar lists of icons (the maple leaf, moose and totem pole of Canada; the eucalyptus, kangaroo and boomerang of Australia, and so on).

Many Kiwiana symbols are also entities that are fun to play with, consume or gaze on, and which are easily transported either physically or as an image. This enables them to operate as devices for hawking the Kiwi ideal around the world. The Japanese tourist who leaves New Zealand armed with replica fluffy sheep, and the homesick Kiwi on O.E. in London who wanders down to the aptly named Kiwifruits shop in the Royal Opera Arcade, Pall Mall, to buy a jar of Vegemite, are but two sides of the same coin. It may appear that as Kiwiana is globally appropriated, the uniqueness of our culture is being eroded — but is it? Most of us closely associate Kiwi culture with the geographical confines of New Zealand. However, if we assume that all culture resides in the individuals who habitually reproduce shared meanings and actions, then our culture is not simply the sum of all that exists within the space of Aotearoa. Nor is it simply the preserve of passport-carrying Kiwis, as many other people around the globe share a similar awareness of the All Blacks, Sir Edmund Hillary and New Zealand lamb. The boundaries of all cultures are genuinely fuzzy if not ethereal. Culture is not bound by time or place. Kiwi culture exists wherever people think and act 'Kiwi'.

> *Unlike Zespri, cultures throughout the world are inevitably fuzzy — their boundaries have never been fixed or inviolable*

This cultural translucence works both ways. Consider the kiwifruit, which from its humble origins as a gooseberry in China became a major New Zealand agricultural export and then a food grown around the world. In America the word *Kiwi* is now used to refer to Kiwifruit and even as slang for a testicle ("He hasn't got the Kiwis to stand up and fight like a man"). The furore in New Zealand that surrounded the worldwide spread of kiwifruit farming, though mostly couched in despairing terms of a heart-rending loss of cultural ownership, had more to do with protecting valuable market shares and associated profits. The latest incarnation of kiwifruit — the golden-fleshed, smooth-skinned Zespri — represents the next attempt to reassert proprietary control over this particular horticultural market.

Unlike Zespri, cultures throughout the world are inevitably fuzzy — their boundaries have never been fixed or inviolable. And, as we boldly enter an epoch of mass and rapid-fire global communication, ranging from tourism to the internet, cultures are becoming ever more universal. As the products of such transnational giants as Coca-Cola, Starbucks and Nike are adopted as global emblems of the Good Life, the demise of culture-specific symbols, values and ideals becomes greater. Are we truly surprised any more to see a !Kung Bushman from the Kalahari desert wearing an Adidas T-shirt or an Inuit child playing with a Buzzy Bee?

Yet symbols of all types still remain potent bearers of ideas and ideals. In Kiwi culture, toast and Weetbix combine to symbolise a healthy breakfast, sandwiches bespeak the ideals of a packed lunch, and a feast of roast lamb and chocolate sauce pudding denotes a winter-warming dinner. Divergences within these generalised schemes can mark a break with formality (cheese on toast for dinner); a different time or social context (a roast for Sunday lunch); or a different ideal (sexual intimacy and chocolate sauce). Cultural ideals may also be contested by counter-symbols. The repeated attacks on the pine tree on One Tree Hill in Auckland were a powerful symbol of Maori resentment towards European imperialism in Aotearoa. Likewise, the younger brother who embarrasses his older sister by bursting through the closed bathroom door whilst she is showering may simply be an inquisitive little scamp with voyeuristic tendencies (a budding anthropologist in the making). Or he could be trying to symbolically belittle his sister's claims to superiority based on advanced age and sexual/physical maturity. Many teenagers who rebel against their parents are also likely to use symbols that directly express counter-values. By adopting a punk rock or gothic lifestyle — symbolised through outrageous clothing and body piercings, ear-splitting music, overt drug-taking and miscreant antics — many consciously resist the order and work ethic typical of many older Kiwis. One of the most ironic teenage rebellions I heard of involved a teenager whose parents were extremely liberal in a post-'60s sort of way and allowed him to regularly use recreational drugs and have his girl-friends stay over on weekends. This teenager rebelled against his parents' world-view by spurning a life of unbridled debauchery and running away to join the Mormon church.

Middle-class Kiwis use — consciously and unconsciously — a wide range of symbols to express many of their class-based ideals and virtues. Consider the Country Road brand of clothing and furnishings. The image is one of order, cleanliness and subtlety, virtues widely exalted by those who share social class and status (and complete lack of imagination). In contrast, those with artistic backgrounds or temperaments are more likely to wear gaudy, flamboyant and home-made clothing, perfect props to any dramatic entrance. The zenith of cultivated and intellectual refinement, however, is displayed by casually owning, but not conceitedly displaying, truly valuable or collectors' items (a McCahon, 1920s Moorecroft pottery or 18th century antiques). Among the moneyed middle classes, flaunting your social status can include leasing or owning a new Series 5 Beamer for about-town use, a near-new Rover Discovery for incarcerating the wife and towing the boat to the Taupo holiday home, and a late-model Honda Civic for the nanny to run household errands. Though this may appear excessive, it is nevertheless the type of symbolic affluence that many Kiwis aspire to.

Ironically, many in the middle classes express their social status by adopting a less-is-more ethos. This is noticeable whenever one of us chooses not to fully use or consume items that our comparative wealth has enabled us to acquire. A strident example is owning large and expensive 4WD vehicles that are never used off-road and regularly lumber around narrow city streets like invading tanks. The ethos also extends to eating, or not eating, as the case may be. Typical middle-class culinary pastimes such as vegetarian or vegan lifestyles, dieting, only eating organic foods, or simply abstaining from eating white bread, serve to symbolise an individual's class-based ability to voluntarily forsake a world of plenty. The ideals of choice, judicious restraint, rational enhancement of wellbeing, and of discreet status expression are all highlighted in the less-is-more symbolism. In contrast, those truly on the breadline will generally eat whatever crumbs are thrown their way.

Like the meanings expressed through language, the ideas expressed through symbols can also be diverse or polysemic (having many meanings). I once built a fence that included trellis windows at regular intervals. The fence denoted the confines of our property and the ideas of social inclusion or exclusion that are commonly linked with territorial boundaries. But for me the trellis windows had other meanings and purposes. Being roughly the size of a domestic television, the trellis windows symbolised how media such as TV promise grand vistas of understanding, but actually restrict our gaze to very narrow outlooks. Secondly, the trellis windows symbolised the fact that boundaries are always partial and never absolute. So, just as a view of our cottage was accessible through the fence, our children could watch the outside world from the relative safety of our garden. The trellis windows also allowed the strong nor'wester through, thereby reducing the strain on the fence and more effectively reducing the speed of the prevailing wind. The fence became quite a talking point in our rural community. Women said they loved it because it was different. Most men — though admitting a grudging respect for the portly academic who had built the fence — would inquire: "Why did you put those bloody holes in it?" People who share a culture will generally agree on core symbolic meanings, though there is no reason they should agree on their varied values, morals or alternative expressions.

In New Zealand (and elsewhere) symbolic dialogues increasingly influence our daily lives. This is partly because our existence is populated by strangers, and symbolic media such as clothing, jewellery, cars and other personal possessions are an ever more effective way to communicate our gender, social status, sexuality and age. Symbols can be easily manipulated to convey different ideas and values, and are therefore extremely useful in rituals. The colour of a wedding dress — whether white, cream or black — can express a range of meanings depending on the situation. But the real masters of the symbolic domain are the advertisers and other marketing types. The hysterical hyperbole that is their daily meat and drink knows no bounds. Core issues of historical fact and social reality are of little moment to these true knights of post-modernity. In the world of advertising a Viking warrior riding a Harley Davidson along Route 66 can just as easily extol the virtues of a Nordic beer brewed in Indonesia, as a Lotto advertisement can proclaim that simply buying a Lucky Dip opens up vistas of fun, sun, leisure and community to the buyer. Similarly Kellogg's Cornflakes — which were originally known as Granose and produced by Dr John Harvey Kellogg in the late 1900s as part of a curative diet for masturbation — have over time been transformed into a byword for morning nutrition and weight-watching. In a complete reversal of the original intent, TV advertisements for Special K strongly hint at the orgasmic pleasures that may be enjoyed through munching pretty much the same baked flakes of corn.

Advertising or branding is used to symbolically differentiate products that are very similar in form and function. The same crude oil that arrives in New Zealand in large tankers is used to supply a variety of distributors, whether Mobil or Challenge. The key point of difference between these petrol distributors — who now all provide extra shopping services and customer loyalty programmes — is their media campaigns. These generally appeal to different environmental, service, or improved-engine-performance sentiments in the hope of luring customers. And it works. The green livery of the BP petrol stations has always hooked me as environmentally friendly, although as a child I thought that Mobil was Catholic petrol (probably because my father regularly filled the car at the local Mobil station after Sunday mass).

Despite — or maybe because of — such marketing fictions we use mass-produced goods daily as markers of our 'unique' personalities. I know a woman who wore Calvin Klein's *Eternity* perfume whenever she despaired of being trapped in her abusive marriage and *Escape* when she believed she might find the strength to break free. After finally leaving her oppressive husband she changed her perfumes to *Be* and *One* to signify her hard-won liberty. A short while later, however, she gave her new lover *Eternity* aftershave and deodorant to express her desire that he not only smell nice, but would love her eternally — thereby demonstrating how we, as consumers, can adroitly employ the same marketing brands and symbolism to express our personal narratives, whatever they may be at any particular time.

In the USA consumers can have their clothing embroidered with distinctive patterns or laser-tattooed with personal designs. Levis stores even provide spa-pools and drying facilities so that self-aware shoppers can shrink their jeans to their unique body dimensions. Nike enables its more discerning customers to show their individuality by having their names or other personal details inscribed on the side of their running shoes. Yet the company refused one customer's request to have the words 'sweat shop' emblazoned on his Nike shoes — proving that even in the *laissez-faire* worlds of commerce and free markets, some expressions of individuality are still over the top.

To be fair, mass-produced commodities have always been able to transcend their economic realities — especially when consumed by culture-bearing human beings, who instil symbolic meaning into everything they possess. When we buy an object at a garage sale it can seem to exist somewhere between a commodity and a personal gift. That the object was once mass-produced and likewise consumed *en masse* is largely overcome by the history and values that specific owners may attribute to the product over time. A couch or a coffee table from Farmers or The Warehouse can become a repository of experiences and memories — the more seemly of which may be disclosed to a potential buyer at a garage sale. If the buyer shows interest in the item's biography, the seller might even be moved to cut the price as they partially gift the product and its stories to the new owner.

Everything that we can imagine, perceive or use is stuffed full with symbolism and associated cultural, social, economic and political consequences. As cultivated animals we are all meaning makers and meaning communicators. As such our everyday worlds are full of talk and symbols … just ask any florist on Valentine's Day.

Take a metaphorical leap into these readings:

Douglas M (1996) *Natural Symbols: Explorations in cosmology*, New York, Routledge

Firth R (1973) *Symbols: public and private*, London, Allen & Unwin

Geertz C (1973) *The Interpretation of Cultures*, New York, Basic Books Inc

Goody J (1993) *The Culture of Flowers*, Cambridge University Press

Herrman G (1997) 'Gift or Commodity: What changes hands in the US garage sale?' in *American Ethnologist*, 24 (4)

Kopytoff I (1986) 'The cultural biography of things: commodization as process' in A Appadurai (ed), *The Social Life of Things: Commodities in cultural perspective*, Cambridge University Press

Levi-Strauss C (1970) *The Raw and the Cooked*, London, Cape

Money J (1985) 'Destroying Angel: Sex, fitness & food' in *The Legacy of Degeneracy Theory: Graham Crackers, Kellogg's Corn Flakes & American Health History*, New York, Prometheus Books

Seguin-Fontes, Marina (2004) *The Language of Flowers*. New York, Sterling Publishing

Turner V (1974) *Dramas, Fields, and metaphors: symbolic action in human society*, Ithaca, Cornell University Press

Williamson J (1978) *Decoding advertisements: ideology and meaning in advertising*, London: Marion Boyars

www.pioneerthinking.com/flowerlanguage.html

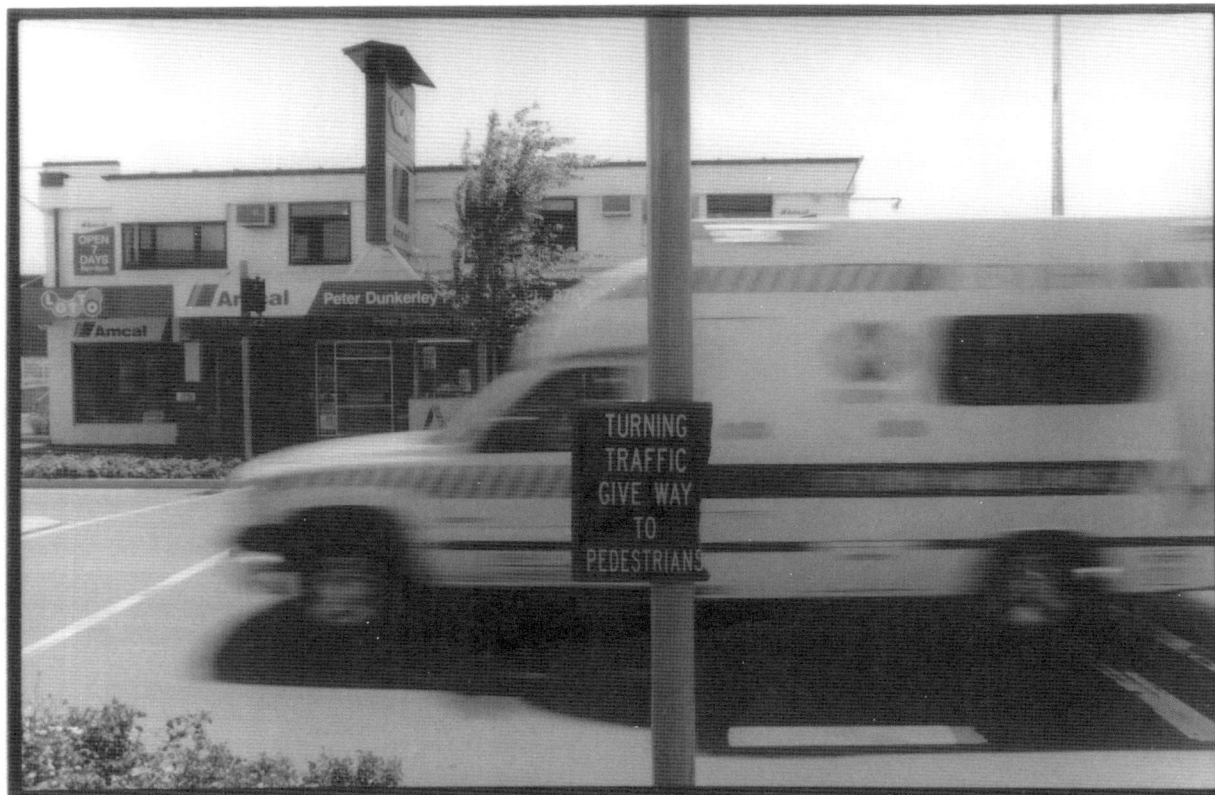

IV

THE NAME OF THE GAME IS LOTTO

GAMBLING, TRANSNATIONALISM, LUCK & IDEAL KIWIS

AFTER FOUR YEARS in Europe I returned to New Zealand in 1989 to find a country obsessed with a weekly, computerised lottery called Lotto. Everywhere I went people talked about what they would do if they won Lotto, this reaching almost frenzied levels as the Saturday draw approached. Their winning dreams customarily included paying off their mortgages, buying new cars, embarking on world holidays or financially assisting members of their extended families. Some fantasised about telling their bosses where to stick it, though most outwardly rejected a Lotto-endowed life of idle affluence on the basis that they "wouldn't know what to do with themselves."

Even my grey-haired mother was hooked. Before my departure she had held firm to the middle-class virtues typical of her generation, especially hard work and sensible spending. She had hitherto avoided most forms of gambling, apart from buying the odd raffle ticket to support the local school or service club. Now she religiously bought a ticket every week and even worked part-time in the local Lotto shop. Mum was clearly enamoured with the prospect of winning — or at least selling a

ticket for — the first division prize. Like many of her era, though, she did have some reservations. She felt that one million dollars was too much money for one person to win and rejoiced whenever the top prize was shared among several people (actually the average first division payout for many years was around $400,000). In fact my mother's Lotto play had become ritualised. She bought her ticket on the same day every week and used the same self-selected numbers, many of which had personal significance as they corresponded with the birth dates of family members. After a busy Saturday's work (50% of all Lotto tickets are bought on this day, and 25% between 5 and 7pm), she would make her weary way home to watch the televised draw at 8pm. Over the years my mum's hopes of winning the first division have been consistently thwarted. However, the occasional thrill of winning a lower division prize, many years' worth of dreams about winning and the knowledge that part of her expenditure has helped worthy causes, have ensured that she is basically happy with Lotto — although she does from time to time tell herself off for continuing to play "such a daft game." In most respects my mum is little different from many other Kiwis. New Zealand's most comprehensive gambling survey recently showed that despite the dramatic growth in casinos and gaming machines, Lotto remains the gambling pastime most of us choose, with 35% of adults (15+) fluttering every week and spending on average $6.86. More than half a million regularly watch the televised draw and 81% of us can apparently recognise a Lotto theme tune without visual prompting. Even several years after my research into Lotto advertising, I still find the *We're in the money* and *Saturday is the name of the day* jingles regularly bouncing around my anthropological brain.

The same survey showed that Lotto players are typical of New Zealand society:

- 51% are female, 49% male
- 79% are Pakeha, 12% Maori, 4% Pacific Island and 3% Asian
- The most likely age of players is 25-34 years (21%), 35-44 years (22%) and 45-54 (18%)
- 70% were employed, 3% were unemployed and 27% were "not in the labour force" (e.g. homemakers, indolent intellectuals)
- 12% had a tertiary degree, 44% a trade qualification, 21% obtained their highest qualification from high school and 22% had no formal qualifications

- 17% earned less than $20,000 per annum and 18% earned $70,001 or more.

Comparing 192 lottery providers worldwide, the New Zealand Lotteries Commission (NZLC) ranked 88th in total sales (US$269m in 2000). The Dai-Ichi Kangyo Bank Lottery in Japan topped the lot with US$7,759m. The top Australian lottery was New South Wales' with total sales of US$517m. In terms of per capita sales Kiwis ranked 82nd with an average individual expenditure of US$70 per annum. This compares with Western Australians who topped the Aussie expenditure at US$133 per annum, and with participants in the Rhode Island Lottery (USA) who ranked as the most profligate in the world at US$879 a year.

50% of all Lotto tickets are bought on Saturday, and 25% between the hours of 5 and 7pm

If you ever wonder how we arrived at such a predicament, simply cast your mind back to July 1987 when six brightly coloured, naturally propelled balls bounced down an isolated country road and across our TV sets. No dialogue was heard, no explanatory narrative was provided. An infant sun rose above a distant, awakening city, while an unseen dog barked at the passing balls. Known in the trade as a teaser, this was the first TV advert for Lotto. Only ten seconds long and seemingly innocuous, it tapped into a host of shared beliefs and values. Firstly, the bouncing balls — which in the Kiwi psyche evoke sentiments of competitive sports such as rugby and cricket —

promoted Lotto as a game that was fun and exciting to play. Although subtle, this message was reinforced by text that appeared in a later version of the advertisement: *Fun and Fortune are bouncing your way … soon.* The balls also appealed to our beliefs about luck, being connected with the idea of 'the bounce of the ball.' The ads implied that Lotto was a game based on luck and not skill. It was promoted as the type of game that everyone could take part in on an equal footing — egalitarian gambling for fair-minded Kiwis.

These ads also sold Lotto as a gift from nature to NZers and therefore as innately good. Lotto's imminent arrival was painted as the triumphal dawn of a better, brighter New Zealand. Other early ads depicted the balls bouncing through a shopping mall and an airport terminal. Lotto — unlike set-apart gambling activities (e.g. TAB betting, see Chapter 8) — was depicted as a normal, everyday consumer activity. As the balls bounced past tired shoppers and world-weary travellers their lives were instantly transformed and they all began jumping up and down with excitement. Clearly Lotto wasn't just any consumer activity, it magically promoted fun and high-energy entertainment. At the same time a narrator, who was none other than the typical arch-critic of gambling, namely an educated middle-class Pakeha woman, told potential consumers how easy it was to play and how pots of prosperity were only a Lucky Dip away. If this feminine protector of all that is wholesome could endorse Lotto then, like Fresh-Up juice in the morning, it had to be good for you. The ads concluded with a happy Pakeha family (including the obligatory labrador) huddled together to watch the draw. Suddenly the family erupted as one, hugging each other in joyous celebration of their win. Lotto is not the mere pursuit of money that it appears — it also promotes harmony and goodwill between ages, genders, ethnic groups and even species.

These were among the first salvoes in the NZLC's war to dis-associate Lotto from other forms of gambling. Depicted as a simple game, participating in, or rather *playing*, Lotto was not gambling, but rather *gaming*. According to the NZLC, Lotto — which involves no skill, all chance, high odds, minimal outlay ($2.40), no age restriction on playing and no real opportunity for immediate reinvestment of winnings — does not contribute to gambling problems. In contrast, pokies, horse races and black-jack encourage people to re-wager any winnings in the mis-guided belief that their individual skills will help them beat the odds. According to many psychologists, it is these types of gambling that cause problems and addict punters. Distinguishing the good of gaming from the evil of gambling is something that the NZLC has invested a lot of energy and money in — to the chagrin of other gambling operators who constantly find themselves labelled as depraved. Irrespective of Lotto's actual effect on problem gambling, many Kiwis have taken this rhetoric to heart and at worst regard Lotto as a benign form of gambling.

Most forms of gambling have always been subject to bad press. They have been accused of encouraging madness, subverting the work ethic, taxing the poor, causing family break-ups and military failure, and even providing a pathological substitute for masturbation (according to Freud, anyway). In New Zealand the first laws against gambling — the 1881 Gaming and Lotteries Act — outlawed all betting and gaming houses, restricted totalisator betting on horse races to on-course only and forbade most lotteries. The Act was part of a concerted effort by the nation's moralists to assert the Protestant work ethic and curb the excesses of male pioneer culture, which commonly included drinking, cursing, singing, illicit sex and gambling. By 1894 the number of horse race meetings had been reduced by one third and in 1907 street bookmaking was declared illegal, together with the advertising of race meetings and the publishing of any tips or dividends. In 1910 all bookmaking was banned and until 1951 there was no legal way to make off-course bets on horse races.

Yet during this time provisions were made for the disposal of certain goods — art works, works of literature, mechanical models and mineral specimens — through lotteries organised by registered, non-profit institutions such as art unions. In 1929 the New Zealand government realised the political and financial rewards that could be gained through lotteries and established its own Art Union lottery that handed out its profits to worthy causes through the Ministry of Internal Affairs. After World War II public interest in the national Art Union lottery waned, yet the demand for lottery profits from bodies as diverse as scientific research institutes and sports clubs continued to grow. In response to this demand and the influence of overseas lotteries, the government introduced the Golden Kiwi lottery in 1961, which offered larger prizes and more frequent draws. Golden Kiwi was an instant hit, though its star also eventually faded and it was abandoned in 1989 to be replaced by an even more dazzling array of state-sponsored gambling including Lotto (1987), Instant Kiwi (1989), Daily Keno (1994), Telebingo (1996–2001), Risk (2001) and PowerBall (2001). By the time Lotto was introduced the die was cast and most of us saw state-run or sponsored lotteries as integral to the Kiwi way of life.

About ten years after Lotto began we witnessed the moving early-morning opening of the national museum, Te Papa. It was proclaimed by commentators as a watershed in the development of a mature national identity and the élite of our society assembled to pay homage. Sir Peter Blake, the much-admired winner of the America's Cup in 1995, officially opened the museum. Standing proud amid this glittering array of the nation's finest was Lotto in the form of a live Superdraw held in the museum foyer. As Lotto money had helped fund Te Papa and Blake's America's Cup campaign the message was clear: Lotto was one of New Zealand's many treasures. What's more, Lotto had the figures on board to back up such a claim: its first year generated a total income of $143 million. By 1997 this had ballooned to $394 million — an increase of 275%, which prompted the NZLC to proudly announce that of the Top 200 New Zealand companies: "The commission is easily the country's most profitable operator in the commercial sector," being ranked 9th for after-tax profits and 30th for total turnover.

Few people are immune from Lotto's influence. Aside from

the millions of participants, the televised draw and advertising, a veritable 'who-wants-what' of worthy community groups get, and in many cases rely on, funding from Lotto profits. By 1997 the NZLC had paid $1 billion to the Lottery Grants Board for charitable dispersal.

So Lotto is not simply a game — it is THE GAME. To an anthropologist this raises the question *why?* Several surveys report that the overwhelming majority — more than 80% — of Lotto regulars do so to win money. But the same surveys do not ask *which* money. Given that many older Kiwis dislike million dollar prizes going to only one individual, we cannot simply presume that the most desired prize is the first division. Indeed, on average only 3% of prizes are left unclaimed each year, which tends to suggest that players desire all Lotto money no matter what the denomination. However, by the end of 2001 there was some $10 million in unclaimed Lotto winnings, of which only three first division prizes accounted for nearly $5 million. The rest was largely made up of thousands of unclaimed fourth/fifth division prizes. This suggests these smaller prizes are of lesser, or even no importance, to many Kiwis. So when you ask someone why they play Lotto and they respond: "You have to be in to win!" you can, with some reservations, assume they mean to win Lotto's first prize. The lure of a large sum for a relatively small outlay is clearly

They have been accused of encouraging madness, subverting the work ethic, taxing the poor, causing family break-ups and military failure, and even providing a pathological substitute for masturbation

appealing. Yet the astronomical odds of winning the first division pre-ordain that, for most, the Lotto experience will be one of repeated loss. The basic logic of profit means that for every Lotto millionaire there are millions more losers. As the NZLC only pays back about 55% in prize money, the most any player can reasonably expect is to lose 45c for every dollar they invest.

Is this reasonable? Well, yes and no. Obviously the 'in-to-win' motto has merit — if you are not in you are never going to win. But most people tend to overestimate their chances of winning. This is partly due to New Zealand's small population, where there are only a few degrees of separation from someone who knows someone who has won Lotto. More to the point, most of us are totally ignorant of the odds of winning the first division prize. The first division odds are 1 in 3,838,380 — considerably worse than picking a winner in the Melbourne Cup (1 in 24) or of being injured while flying with the world's safest airline, Canada Air (1 in 1.3 million). These astronomical odds are beyond our everyday comprehension. What these actually mean is that if you spent $6 a week on Lotto for 60 years (total expenditure $18,720), taking care to select different numbers every time, you will only ever buy 0.823% or 31,200 of all the possible 3.8 million combinations. To calculate the odds of winning Lotto PowerBall, simply multiply these figures by eight!

Now, I've done the sums and I know the odds, yet most weeks I — like untold other Kiwis — buy a Lotto ticket. So if most of us who play are 'in-to-win,' yet winning is stubbornly elusive, what exactly are we winning that keeps us in? Aside from keeping our dreams of winning alive, participating in Lotto also provides other fulfilments that can help maintain our interest. High among these are the small wins, the second and lower division prizes. Winning such a prize can create a sense of financial gain, but more importantly it promotes ideas of luck. Many players who win a lower division prize believe that their luck is in, that they are on a roll. I've met people who have worn the same socks or repeated the same ticket-buying rituals in the hope of retaining — or even enhancing — their luck for the next week's draw. As expected, their efforts came to nothing as Lotto numbers are drawn according to pure, random chance. Belief in luck is pervasive in our culture and the NZLC advances such notions when they promote 'lucky number boards' in Lotto outlets and 'lucky Lotto shops' such as the Peter Dunkerley Chemist in Hastings. Many punters have lucky numbers they use every week for their self-selected tickets, which account for some 30% of tickets sold. This strategy can lead to what psychologists call 'entrapment' — a state where, because of your long-term investment in the same numbers, you become afraid of missing a draw in case those numbers come up. With typical marketers' cheek, this apparently harmful state of affairs is now used to promote Lotto under the banner *Never miss a week. Never miss a draw* — with ads showing hapless saps humiliated for forgetting to buy their ticket.

Often lucky numbers are the birthdates of family members and loved ones. In selecting these a player may recreate a unique sense of self. I used to think I was the only person who chose '1,2,3,4,5,7' when playing Lotto. I thought most people would not choose sequential numbers in the erroneous belief that 'spread-out' numbers had more chance of winning. Just in case someone did, I included the '5-7' hiccup. When I told this to a NZLC rep she smiled kindly and then dispelled my illusion of individualistic grandeur, explaining that they got dozens of entries like it every week.

In everyday life we are encouraged to create a distinct expression of self through acts of public consumption. Lotto, however, is not open to the same public scrutiny or censure that other forms of conspicuous behaviour may attract (e.g. eating with your mouth open). The shared acts and beliefs of most Lotto players are hidden from one another. Thousands watch the live draw on a Saturday night and most suffer the same let-down — week in, week out. Alone with their shattered dreams, the most obvious response for the frustrated player is not to engage in a structural analysis of the lottery, but simply to conclude that it simply wasn't *their* lucky week.

Lotto has other paybacks, too. For some isolated elderly people, buying a ticket allows them to enjoy social contact with Lotto retailers. For others it's a way to contribute to worthy causes. This is especially true for women, who make up 51% of Lotto players (a very high proportion for gambling activities, which are generally dominated by males). Although Lotto philanthropy appears to be based on individual 'greed' rather than social altruism, many of us consider that playing Lotto is comparable with buying a ticket in a community raffle to show support for the local school or scout group. Yet with Lotto's charity the community that benefits is New Zealand society at large, and therein lies the rub.

As an extremely popular and fun activity — renowned for supporting good causes and widely seen as divorced from pathological gambling — Lotto potentially reveals what types of gambling are seen as ideal or positive in our culture. But Lotto is also a state-sanctioned activity. The New Zealand government is a major stakeholder in Lotto, having passed the 1977 Gaming and Lotteries Act which established the NZLC. Besides collecting taxes from sales, the state was directly represented on the NZLC board until 1999 by the Secretary of Internal Affairs, and the board still reports to the Minister. The Department of Internal Affairs also provides the policy and logistic support for the New Zealand Lottery Grants Board. What political agendas, then, may be served by Lotto's continued success?

Think for a moment about the TV ads on the theme of *Saturday is the name of the day and Lotto is the name of our game.* They depicted numerous characters — typical New Zealanders and home-grown celebrities — in an array of activities commonly linked with the Kiwi Saturday, from swimming, playing golf and BBQs, to getting married. All the activities featured characters buying a Lotto ticket and concluded with diverse groups gathering to watch the live draw. The draw itself was not shown, nor was anybody winning. Unlike earlier commercials that promoted winning as the prime reason for involvement, these later ads implied that merely playing Lotto was its own reward. In one, entertainer Howard Morrison happily stuck his losing ticket on his forehead, letting it blow away in the wind, and cricketer Jeremy Coney laughingly ate his losing ticket after enjoying a round of golf. The ads sought to align Lotto with Saturday — an iconic day in our Good Life psyche, filled with sun-drenched leisure by beach, lake or river and populated with varied, creative individuals playing in a dynamic state of egalitarian harmony and social goodwill. The ads depicted Lotto as the enabling ritual of the Good Life and the simple purchase of a Lucky Dip affirmed an individual's membership in the Good Life club. All Lotto players are by definition good Kiwis, just as all good Kiwis play Lotto. Although winning Lotto may secure you a bigger slice of the Good Life pie, it is our unadulterated commitment to playing THE GAME — to being a good Kiwi — that really counts!

Lotto's variant, PowerBall, hits all these spots. Firstly, it was promoted through the series of 'Count me in' advertisements. These emphasised that in playing PowerBall you were validating your membership in the fun-loving, perpetually sunny and ever-harmonious society of Kiwidom. PowerBall also offers a potential life-changing prize — many millions in fact. Yet a cunning twist of structural logistics, namely the synthesis of the huge odds against winning and the automatic PowerBall jackpot after reaching $30 million, means that the first prize is usually shared between the multiple winners of lower divisions. In April 2001 the $9.9 million PowerBall prize was not struck by any ticket in the first or second divisions and was shared among 78 winners of the third division, who each got $127,907. This structure ensures that the potential vastness of PowerBall first-division prize never completely overwhelms. At a certain level it supports the ethos of egalitarianism while at the same time promoting the middle-class tenet of personal advancement. Though many older Kiwis would be uncomfortable if individuals repeatedly won millions in PowerBall, they positively dance in the streets if twenty or more people each win $500,000.

Many New Zealanders share the belief that Lotto is a game for ordinary Kiwis. They think that individuals like Bob Jones and other wealthy people should not be allowed to play. Neither, do they think, should anyone who has previously won Lotto, unless of course they are willing to give their 'extra' winnings to charity. One elderly woman tried to return her share of the first division as she felt that winning had morally excluded her from further involvement and that this effectively ruled out her weekly visit to the local Lotto shop. Similarly the fantasies of many players centre on simply securing what they already own or can reasonably expect to aspire to in their lifetimes (e.g. paying off the mortgage, buying a new boat). In this respect Lotto is thought of as the ordinary Kiwi's chance

> *Lotto is ... the ordinary Kiwi's chance to secure — but not necessarily transcend — their personal piece of the Good Life paradise*

to secure — but not necessarily transcend — their personal piece of the Good Life paradise. Advertisers have been quick to idealise this egalitarian ethos and even depict winners as simple, quirky folk. Remember the chubby lawnmower rider, the lithe dolphin-swimmer and, most charmingly, the young hipsters who spurn café society to give their winnings to worthy rural charities? No fast-cars or champagne for our spontaneously wealthy winners. Flamboyant big-noting is simply not part of our ideal cultural heritage.

Lotto is plainly being used to promote utopian ideals of nationhood. The parallels between its rhetoric and the idealistic statements about New Zealand society so beloved of post-war politicians are quite startling. Ultimately it is a case of buy a Lucky Dip and help maintain New Zealand as a truly caring, sharing, dynamic and sun-drenched society. But our beloved lottery is much more than simply a local phenomenon, it is also part of a rapidly expanding global gambling industry. Indeed, a current trend in anthropology looks at links between seemingly insignificant, everyday and home-based occurrences and the much broader structures of world economics and politics. This reflects the increasingly global influences in our lives. When the price of milk on international markets is up — and local farmers are getting a better deal offshore — there is a corresponding domestic price rise.

Thus, Lotto is not simply filling the mythical void left by the demise of one-nation, one-people politics; it also works to serve the interests of transnational economics. Many of us are unaware that Lotto is only one of many state-sponsored lotteries that support a burgeoning global industry of lottery providers that was worth US$128,139 million in year 2000. GTECH provided lottery computer technology in New Zealand and in at least 26 American, four Australian and three Canadian states; 23 European, three Asian, five South American, three African and five Caribbean countries, as well as in Mexico and Israel. Meanwhile, advertising moguls Saatchi & Saatchi were the creative genius behind lottery advertising in America, Australia, Great Britain and New Zealand. Armed with such knowledge, it may also be judicious to ask how Lotto works in the interests of transnational companies, beyond their obvious pursuit of profit.

These companies rely on the quick movement of people, knowledge and capital across state boundaries. Their financial interests may conflict with the more geographically bound or territorial concerns of the nation-state. This potential for conflict is not glib scaremongering. Of the world's top 100 economies, 51 are transnationals, while only 49 are actual countries. Taking the top 20 economies in year 2000, nine were transnationals, the highest-ranking being General Motors at number eight. Unsurprisingly the good ol' USA was numero uno. The 12th largest economy was Wal-Mart, which generated an annual revenue greater than that of 161 countries including New Zealand, Israel, Poland and Greece. The cigarette manufacturer Philip Morris, which operates in 170 countries but does not even rank in the top 100 companies, is itself economically bigger than New Zealand. The combined sales of the world's top 200 corporations accounted for more than a quarter of the world's economic activity, and, with more than 40,000 of them worldwide, the balance of economic-political power appears to be inevitably shifting in their favour. Yet in Lotto we glimpse how nation-states and transnational corporations can resolve their potential conflicts and work together to support each other's ideals.

Firstly, transnationals have actively negotiated key alliances with different countries to ensure that their combined activities create a compliant labour force and stimulate wealth through increased consumer activity. Since Lotto was introduced we have experienced:

- The economic and political machinations of Rogernomics
- The 1991 Employment Contracts Act and the demise of union muscle
- An increase in foreign ownership — now well over 50% of shares listed on the New Zealand Stock Exchange are owned by overseas investors (up from 19% in 1989)
- The privatisation of state-owned resources including electricity supply, railways, telecommunications, state banks and insurance companies, Air New Zealand (now bought back and saved from potential financial ruin) and others
- More of the country's top companies locating themselves offshore

■ Deregulated markets and the removal of tariffs on imported goods to encourage competitive global trade (with the loss of local jobs).

Secondly, transnationals have advanced nationalist sentiments through the localised branding of their products. Remember the Japanese car manufacturer, Toyota, and their 'Welcome to my world' and 'Everyday People' advertising campaigns? These featured sublime local landscapes and a colourful cast of Kiwi characters — including the Asian market gardener who pronounces at the end "Every day I think this is a gwate [sic] place … yeah." Now in 2004 it's the turn of the overseas-owned ANZ bank to claim they're us. They are, of course, but not simply in the way they portray in their televisions ads. Yes, they are New Zealand's first commercial bank, and yes they are staffed by a diverse group of 'Kiwis', but their foreign owners are just as much a part of our culture as the soap opera *Shortland Street*. Cultures are not fixed in time or place and ANZ, like Dr Ropata, exist on both sides of the Tasman and elsewhere.

The social and financial ideals of transnationalism — where every citizen has the ordained right to aspire to the American Dream — have come under fire as repeated cycles of economic boom'n'bust have proven that hard work, prudent investment and wise spending are not necessarily enough to guarantee individual success. Transnational companies have responded by

In many respects Lotto is reminiscent of the Melanesian cargo cults which proliferated after World War II in response to colonial rule and oppression.

actually celebrating the unpredictability of economic and social environments. Although they have counselled us to strive for a better life, they have also recognised that many factors beyond our control can dramatically change our circumstances. For example, house and contents insurance premiums in New Zealand can rise due to damage caused by tornados across North America and the losses sustained by global insurance companies.

So transnationals — and many nation-states, as evidenced by the growing number of state-operated or sponsored lotteries around the world (195 at last count) — have promoted risk-taking and luck as ideals. Which may explain why the sight of middle-aged, middle-class males — concerned about losing their edge in business and between the sheets — cavorting around the countryside bungy-jumping, tandem skydiving and paragliding is now quite common. Many of us now believe that the gap between our present circumstances and future prosperity will not necessarily be achieved by sober, hard grind but rather will be made in a single lucky leap. Hence the great weight we attach to risk-taking and the need for luck … and the widespread popularity of lotteries.

As Lotto 'play' is mainly an experience of repeated loss, players are conversely taught to be happy with their current lot in life, but also to keep taking risks in the hope of achieving a better future. Playing Lotto disciplines Kiwis to remain committed to the Game of Life — win, lose or draw. The unpredictability of success or failure in such a game of chance also advances the idea that our fate chiefly depends on luck. In a parallel situation a racehorse in Japan, Haru-urara, became a national hero after losing a hundred consecutive races. The Japanese prime minister declared "It's a nice story that gives people hope that they shouldn't give up even if they lose." Ardent fans punt on the horse knowing it will lose, then keep the dud tickets as good luck charms.

Lotto's moral message places the burden of success squarely on the individual and thereby deflects focus away from the fact that Lotto — like life generally today — is structured to ensure there will be more losers than winners. Lotto promotes an atmosphere in which many of us believe a better life is only six numbers away and where critical analysis of the social, economic and political inequities that basically predetermine our lot is to be avoided. Any negative feelings we may have about consistently losing are diluted by the celebration of the Kiwi Good Life as an ideal and of the game's total outputs — dynamic players, lucky winners and an altruistic society.

In many respects Lotto is reminiscent of the Melanesian cargo cults that proliferated after World War II in response to colonial rule and oppression. They have been maintained ever since by devotees convinced that if they perform the 'rituals' of wartime Europeans — such as marching in straight lines — boatloads of cargo (e.g. tinned foodstuffs) will magically appear and they will forever be freed from hard toil. When the cargo doesn't arrive the cultists do not ditch their core beliefs, they just change their leaders or rituals, in much the same way that unlucky players may change their numbers. Cargo cults, like Lotto, promise a future Golden Age whilst conferring culturally appropriate meaning and value to current hard times. And with few of us having rich, near-death relatives and money trees long since proven to be fictitious, subscribing to the cargo cult of Lotto is one way of maintaining our dream of the Good Life. Although if you happen to spot a Dani from Irian Jaya wandering around the Remuera shopping precinct flashing a gold Amex and sporting a rather splendid gold-plated penis sheath, then the illusions of Lotto and the cargo cult may have converged into reality for at least one lucky individual.

In November 2002 the Lotteries Commission introduced a new prize structure to Lotto — the Guaranteed Millionaire. This was in response to the fall in profits that had troubled the NZLC since 1998. Under this new regime if there is only one first division winner they automatically win a million dollars. However, if there are more than one — or indeed no first division winners — an additional draw is held to select a Guaranteed Millionaire. The commission also introduced an additional winning bonus number, thereby increasing the chances of winning a lower division prize. This initiative has been reinforced by one-off draws for Holden Monaro and VW Beetle cars won by random ticket holders.

At the same time Lotto's advertising increasingly focused on the joys of winning this sure-fire prize. Under the general banner of *Lotto — Anything's Possible*, newspaper, radio and television ads make a big play of the certain million-dollar prize: "Imagine the chance to be a millionaire every week! As easy as Lotto." However, similar motifs are still employed — especially those that stress how Lotto can save people from the grind of everyday life, liberating them to bask in the perpetual warmth of the New Zealand Good Life.

In an animated television ad a small, unhappy cog in a large, dark factory is shown breaking free from its mechanical torture and scampering away to the idyllic freedom of the countryside. Here it is welcomed by cheerful daffodils which — in rotating motions that mimic the cog's previous entrapment — wipe away the grime that coats its body. It is thus returned to its original golden lustre, which brilliantly reflects the dazzling sunshine in which it now bathes. Then the little cog — emancipated from all traces of work-related tyranny — hops aboard a sailboat and uses its innate talents to start the rack and pinion system that sets the boat's sail. This completed, it takes charge of the wheel to set a course towards a setting (or rising?) sun, which has the lines *A millionaire every week. What would you do?* written underneath. All this is underscored by Vera Lynn's wartime hit 'Wish me luck as you wave me goodbye' — a touching song that conveyed the departing soldiers' heartfelt desire for upbeat support as they left to confront the horrors of war. In the Lotto ad, however, the situation is reversed as the lucky cog asks those left behind in the trenches of everyday drudgery to wish it luck as it determinedly escapes to the land of Lotto/ Godzone idealism.

This new promotional emphasis — backed by the sure-fire reality of one lucky cog per week — may be working. In the last quarter (April–June) of the 2002–2003 financial year Lotto earnings jumped $14.4m from the previous quarter, although whether this will mark a long-term change in Lotto's fortunes remains to be seen. Don't be surprised if the NZLC starts up a 'Lotto millionaires club' before too long — where hopefully we'll meet again.

Try your luck with a dip into these references:

Abbott M & R Volberg (2000) *Taking the pulse on gambling and problem gambling: A report on phase one of the 1999 National Prevalence*, Wellington, Department of Internal Affairs

Barnet R & J Cavanagh (1994) *Global Dreams: Imperial Corporations and the New World Order*, New York, Simon & Schuster — see also www.globalpolicy.org

Brenner R & G (1990) *Gambling and Speculation: A theory, a history and a future of some human decisions*, Cambridge University Press

Comaroff J & J (2000), '2000 Millennial Capitalism: First Thoughts on a Second Coming' *Public Culture*, 12(2): 291–343

Grant D (1994) *On a Roll: A History of Gambling & Lotteries in New Zealand*, Wellington, Victoria University Press

Howland P (1994) 'Benign Gambling to the New Zealand Good Life: Lotto Television Adverts from 1987 to 1992' *New Zealand Journal of Media Studies*, 1(2):46-58

— (2001) 'Toward an Ethnography of Lotto' *International Gambling Studies*, 1 (Sept): 7-25

— (2002) 'A Lucky Dip? The fun, excitement and collusive hegemony of Lotto,' in B Curtis (ed), *Gambling in New Zealand*, Palmerston North, Dunmore Press

Hyde V (1990) 'Lotto's A Chancy Matter' *New Zealand Science Monthly* December: 12-14

Kelsey J (1995) *The New Zealand Experiment: A World Model for Structural Adjustment?* Auckland University Press

Rouse R (1995) 'Thinking though Transnationalism: Notes on the Cultural Politics of Class Relations in the Contemporary United States' *Public Culture* 7: 353-402

Walker M (1992) *The Psychology of Gambling*, New York, Pergamon Press

V

KIWI SEX —
DITHERING BETWEEN LUST AND CONSTRAINT

SEX

ONE EVENING I WAS sitting in a bar with a group of male friends who had ventured down from the lofty heights of academia to observe the exotic Friday night rituals of the downtown suits. We were quietly enjoying a beer when a young female lurched towards us, cast a discerning eye across our table and in a tone worthy of Marilyn Monroe announced, "I love men!" We were taken aback. As earnest young academics we were reasonably well-versed in feminist theory and knew that anyone uttering such a sentiment in the hallowed halls of academia would be immediately branded a heretic and cast from the cloisters. My companions quickly concluded that the woman was deranged and drunk. I, however, was intrigued.

Sex in its infinite cultural and historical guises is a staple of anthropology, so I invited the woman to join us for a drink, slipped into the empathetic mode of the curious anthropologist and began to gently quiz her. Over the course of the evening she revealed that she really only loved one man in particular — her live-in partner of several years. She was, however, desperately unhappy about the state of their sexual relationship and confided that in the past 18 months they had experienced "only 13 seconds worth of sex" as her partner had developed a problem with premature ejaculation and was unwilling to engage in intercourse, seek help or explore other ways of lovemaking. Rather perversely he compounded this sad state of affairs by actually bragging in public that they enjoyed a wonderful sex life.

This woman's tale is all too common among New Zealand's middle classes, where sex is often expressed as a series of contradictions between public and private; rhetoric and reality; barroom boasts and bedroom failures. Sex is still a relatively taboo subject in Aotearoa, even in a context of changes where prostitution has been decriminalised. Sex shops hide behind painted-out windows, sexologists (theoretical and practical) are thin on the carpet, and meaningful sexual dialogue, especially between males and females, is fraught with incomprehension, mutual antagonism, or is completely absent. A former brothel manager told me she was constantly surprised by the inability of Kiwi males to express their specific sexual needs or even to discuss sex in general. In the realms of commercial sex, money may enable the walk but it doesn't necessarily help the talk. Caught between lust and shame, many males resort to maligning those they profess to love — ask any woman deemed to have failed to fulfil the competing roles of mother, wife, companion and concubine.

Sex itself is mostly conducted in private, beyond public scrutiny. Anthropology's main way of gathering data — participant-observation in people's lives — has obvious drawbacks in the study of sex. Not only can the presence of an anthropologist unduly influence your sexual activity, but holding a torch and taking notes whilst ensconced under a squeaking mattress is technically very demanding. Hence much of my thesis is based on people's talk about sex, which may contain any number of lies, omissions or misunderstandings.

The pursuit of sex is significantly idealised in everyday life. It is a mainstay of advertising; the adulatory stuff of celebrities featured in magazines; and it emboldens the personal columns of such gay-oriented publications as *Up* and *NZGay.com*, much to the delight of bent and straight alike. We often assume that sex *per se* is innately good and desirable, while good sex is even better. If you aren't doing it, getting it or giving it, then you are a personal failure. Never mind that this ethos is unlike the reality of many individuals. A recent study in the US found that younger women and older men often endure persistent 'sexual dysfunction.' Many young women reported that their sex lives were physically, emotionally and socially unsatisfying. The old boys simply complained about their lack of physical prowess.

Challenges to the 'sex is innately good' standard do exist in anonymous letters to agony aunts and whispered confidences between friends. Yet many people still believe that most sexual problems can be overcome by simply snaring the 'right' partner. In Jane Campion's widely acclaimed film *The Piano*, the mute, sexually suppressed female lead is only orgasmically liberated once she has escaped the lovelorn clasp of her uptight Brit and falls, in true Mills & Boon style, into the arms of the nearest half European/half Native — an authentic Pakeha in one of the oldest senses of the word. The idea that a hard man is good to find pervades TV shows such as *Sex in the City*, which supposedly celebrate the sexual freedom of today's women. In one episode the most chaste of the still-single female characters discovers that a vibrator provides her with the most satisfying sex she has ever had. Yet her friends determinedly drag her away from pleasures mechanical and literally push her back towards the enlightened quest for the perfect man.

Most of us meekly agree with the sex-is-good mantra. Those who dare to question the idea that sex is innately good may be ridiculed or seen as failures. As a result many people will put up with a great deal of sexual, physical and emotional discomfort before they have the courage to admit to, let alone change, the circumstances of their intimacy. Yet these standards are not set in stone. I knew a woman who summoned the courage to counter her husband's boastful claims of passionate, almost-nightly sexual gymnastics by publicly stating that his penis felt like ice. Then she quietly reflected on the years of coerced sex and other abuse she had endured at his hands, and the copious amounts of baby oil needed to ensure that their brief sexual encounters were not unbearably painful. And yes, you guessed it — her husband branded her as frigid! She eventually broke free from his icy clutches and went on to luxuriate in a sex life that once included 20+ consecutive orgasms in one afternoon of lovemaking. She soon reached a state of such constant ecstasy that she would immediately climax whenever her new-found love whispered sweet everythings in her ear. Clearly hope springs eternal and glaciers evaporate, yet it appears that too many of us are trapped between the simultaneous celebration and fear of sex, between lust and loathing, truth and lies. While the French and Italians may enjoy reputations as passionate romantics, Kiwis simply flounder between desire and distress, as shown by the aftermath of the infamous 2am nightclub grab (i.e. of anyone left). If you (or your children) have ever woken up wondering who's that in bed with you/them, just what happened between the sheets, then done the early morning walk-of-shame home in party gear, you'll know what I mean.

Compare this with the US, where the public debate on sex is more polarised. Many Americans ascribe to fundamentalist Christian beliefs and think of sex as a proto-shameful act that should only be discharged within the sanctuary of marriage and for the purpose of producing a child. In contrast, many Americans consider sex to be goddamn great and reverently adhere to an almost constitutional belief in the liberating influence of recreational sex. Members of this group enthusiastically patronise swingers clubs, Hooters bars, brothels and an ever-expanding pornography industry. Depending on your personal bent, sex in the US may be a stairway to God or a Saturday night singles bar. For either side there is little middle ground — although this is doubtless the realm in which many Americans experience sex. Flip-flopping between these two extremes is frowned upon. Bible-belters believe that sexual ditherers lack the necessary moral fortitude to walk the straight and narrow, while those committed to the doctrines of liberated sex see them as irritating hypocrites, dreary voyeurs or simply as being in denial.

Not only can the presence of an anthropologist unduly influence your sexual activity, but holding a torch and taking notes whilst ensconced under a squeaking mattress is technically very demanding.

A word of qualification. Heterosexual, homosexual, bisexual, category-defying sexual, ethnic, gender, class and individual experiences of sex will vary within any given culture. For example, many male homosexuals are more sexually knowledgable and technically skilled than their hetero counterparts. Sex is open currency in the homosexual community and Kiwi queers appear vastly more willing to discuss and explore — some would say flaunt — their sexuality than your average (straight) bloke. Queer dating ads leave very little to the imagination, with every inconceivable sexual act, fetish and deviance publicised —

although conversion from metric to inches is sometimes required. Straight personals detailing height, Zodiac sign and a sense of humour are staid by comparison. This may be because homosexual relationships are not so often infused with the unequal physical, economic or social power that can undermine heterosexual liaisons.

Although sex may appear to be a biological phenomenon, with similar body parts going up and down throughout the world, it is also a cultural and historical construct. The advice to many generations of Western women to 'lie back and think of England' was historically prescriptive. Before the free-love movement of the 1960s, and the sexual revolution that continues to this day, many women were condemned to dutifully endure — not necessarily enjoy — sex. Many suffered constant discomfort. Few delighted in orgasms, while fewer still openly discussed their carnal disquiet. It simply wasn't considered a proper topic of conversation, not even with husbands or lovers. Compare this with New Zealand women today, who are constantly encouraged by *Cleo, Cosmopolitan* and a chorus of other sex-is-great messengers to relish in as many orgasms, partners (male and female) and positions as they can possibly manage on a Friday night.

Sex can also vary enormously between cultures. Melanesian sexual beliefs and practices range from the idea that the vitality of a foetus is ensured by many clansmen having repeated intercourse with a pregnant woman, to the belief that conception is caused by ancestral spirits. The Sambia (a pseudonym used by the anthropologist Gilbert Herdt to protect their real identities) of Papua New Guinea are famous in anthropology for their antagonistic gender relations and elaborate, hierarchical system of ritualised homosexuality. Around the age of seven, boys are taken away from their mothers to live in the men's house where they are initially socialised to believe that female sexuality poses a constant threat to male vitality. Then as teenagers they are initiated into ritualised homosexuality — firstly as fellators and later as fellateds — in the belief that swallowing semen will ensure they mature and grow strong. Adult Sambia women are similarly exhorted to ingest semen to strengthen their bodies for child-bearing and to ensure nutritious breast milk.

As married adults Sambia males retain the belief that semen is a scarce and sacred resource that is lost to women through acts of intercourse, which they space apart to ensure they do not age prematurely and die. The Ilahita Arapesh of New Guinea have an even greater fear of female pollutants. After heterosexual intercourse adult males undergo a series of purification rituals that culminate in blood-letting. This involves the male thrusting a barbed cane in a sawing motion up his urethra to ensure that blood flows from his erect penis and any female pollutants are washed away in the river. Some of us simply pee like the doctor recommends.

Though it is doubtful whether blood-letting will ever catch on in Remuera or Fendalton, it is evident that specific sex beliefs and practices are always directly connected to other social processes (gender, age roles, etc). Sexual dithering in New Zealand may be linked to a long history of rural settlement and pastoral morality. Although significantly colonised from the 1830s, New Zealand is distinctive in that most of its populace was still living in rural settlements until 1911. In rural outposts, among the indigenous Maori and in emerging cities such as Auckland and Wellington, many male pioneers eagerly pursued an 'unholy trinity of vice' — alcohol, gambling and illicit sex. Yet by the late 19th century, bookmakers, brothels and bootleggers had been all but outlawed. So effective was the moral backlash that the six o'clock closing of pubs, which had been introduced as a temporary wartime measure in 1917, was not rescinded until 1967.

In their defence, many pioneers lived a liminal existence, which sometimes resulted in the wholesale inversion of the values they had upheld in Mother England. They were literally caught between the bush of Aotearoa and the civilisation of Britain; between breaking in and living off the land. In the bush was the wilderness in its primal sense. Across the sea was civilised society, the epitome of which were the ethics and moralities prescribed (but not necessarily practised) by upper-class Britain. And somewhere in between were the Maoriland pioneers wrestling to establish rural communities. The pioneers' whoring, casual interracial sexual liaisons and other lascivious habits outraged missionaries and other colonial moralists. In Western societies, rural places are often cast as sites of high virtue where work is honest and fruitful, families toil in harmony and communities are maintained by social morality. In trying to bring the natives out of the bush and simultaneously fix wayward pioneers in pastoral society, the missionaries preached that God's favour would be granted if the populace embraced Christian ideals. The moralists persuasively argued that unless sex was limited to wholesome marriage, the social cohesion of New Zealand's emerging society could not be guaranteed.

All of this is ironic because rural folk are constantly surrounded by sex in nature. The entire agricultural enterprise is an attempt to manage 'sex in nature' for our material benefit — from selectively breeding cows with greater milk capacity to raising an heir for the family farm. Rural people share the ethos that sex is an integral part of all existence, animal and human. They also know that their efforts to dominate nature won't always work. Whenever we appear to gain the upper hand, nature is just as likely to wipe out a crop in an unseasonable storm as it is to render a prize stallion infertile. My observations are that rural folk understand that individuals will sometimes stray from the moral path originally laid down by missionaries. By virtue of necessity heirs are sometimes conceived beyond the marital bed, and seasonal influences — such as springtime — can be overwhelmingly seductive. Yet they also understand the need for social cohesion and that unbridled sexuality will eventually threaten the harmony of any rural community — so they compromise. On one hand they publicly aspire to the moral ideals of pastoral sexuality: they attend church, they publicly rebuke individuals who stray from the marital bed and they openly castigate the promiscuous — especially women. With the other hand they accept that such standards cannot always be upheld in private.

The potential conflict between private lust and public constraint is subtle but pervasive. Silences punctuate discussions of immoral carnal activity, amidst a tacit understanding of the realities of sex — especially when it involves rural men. While many believe that men have natural sexual drives that demand relief, the sexuality of rural women is kept on a much tighter leash. This is partly because women are thought of as being closer to nature due to their inherent ability to give birth and physically nurture.

It is a common cross-cultural belief that female sexuality, unless restrained by civilising forces — namely men, marriage and raising children — is potentially disruptive to cohesive social order. In other words, a sexually uninhibited woman doesn't cook, wash or mend and she is likely to tempt men from their rightful work in the fields. The less socially desirable a rural woman is — that is, not connected to the right family or land — the more likely it is that she will be pressed into the service of any male whose sexual urges cannot be adequately discharged within the marital bed. Hence the line between the girls you marry and the farm-maidens who work overtime in the hay shed. In what is hardly a unique historical or cultural example, this imbalance serves to maintain a certain social (and sexual) harmony. If illicit sexual activity ever seriously threatens the cohesion of a rural family or community, gossip networks are quickly activated and punishments — from social ostracism to a thumping behind the local hotel — are meted out.

The rural influence on Kiwi sexuality continued long after we became a fully-fledged urban society. In 1954 the Mazengarb Report was sent to every New Zealand home to warn of the perils of unbridled teenage sexual activity — and all because a few young people in Naenae were having a wild time drinking and sleeping around. The Mazengarb Report postdates Margaret Mead's original treatise on the benefits of relaxed attitudes towards adolescent sexual activity — *Coming of Age in Samoa* — by some 26 years. It also postdates the first *Playboy* magazine, published in the US in 1953, and was contrived a tick before the beginning of the free-love revolution in the '60s. In reality there has always been illicit sex in our cities — from backstreet brothels and ship girls to rent boys. But to this day many of New Zealand's urban middle classes continue to publicly ascribe to agrarian morality while gleefully enjoying illicit sex behind closed doors.

Times are changing and matters sexual in New Zealand are now more openly discussed, debated and sometimes even celebrated. Sex education in my schooldays was slipped almost furtively into the curriculum and consisted of little more than a series of dire health warnings. In comparison my daughter's Year 6 class were encouraged to draw colourful pictures of their gender's genitalia which were then proudly displayed on the classroom walls. Yet while the sexual dialogue may be more open, the politics of phallocentrism still hold fast. Where the girls' drawings were subtle and bordering on the naive, the boys' were positively rampant and depicted impossibly large, resplendent phalluses volcanically erupting in psychedelic orgies of colour.

And although the methods of sex education have clearly changed, New Zealand still records some of the highest rates of unplanned teenage pregnancies and STDs in the West. Once again the pervasive lust/shame complex of our culture appears to dominate, hampering discussion and safe sex among the young.

From Queer Balls to Erotic Exhibitions, concepts of normative sex in New Zealand have shifted from the missionaries' ideals of marital intercourse. For some, anything now goes as long as it's between consenting adults who do not unduly harm each other in the process. Though free will in matters sexual is laudable, its practice is somewhat more problematic. It cannot be assumed that once individuals pass the age of consent they will equally be able to freely match their personal desires with their sexual experiences. Differences in biology, economics and social status can all muddy the waters of sexual equality. Many women who lie back and think of their physical or financial vulnerability are seldom heard to utter the word 'no.' Their voices are simply too small. Moreover, sex often contains hidden agendas. The world of net-sex, for instance, appears to democratically cater for every conceivable passion from necrophilia to plaster-cast fetishes, the immense to the diminutive, the hirsute to the hairless. Imagination, desire and fulfilment achieve climatic union within the matrix of the internet. But the net — just like movies, TV and literature — exists mainly in a world of rhetoric and illusion. It has no necessary link with reality. Images of body parts, acts and events can be digitally manipulated — inflated, deflated and imaginatively twisted to their ideal forms. The women of the internet are achingly carnal, perpetually smiling and forever taut of body, while the men are magnificently enormous and permanently erect. Ironically, if you choose to exit a sex site at the contents-may-offend page, you are often transferred to sites such as Walt Disney, thereby swapping one illusory world for another.

> *The women of the internet are achingly carnal, perpetually smiling and forever taut of body, while the men are magnificently enormous and permanently erect*

The political economy of net-sex also transcends concerns about who can afford to run a computer or whether individuals are compelled by unfortunate circumstance to perform on net-sex sites. Simply try and find a completely free net-sex site. I am no computer geek, but my hours of searching revealed only a handful, compared to the thousands of commercial sites. Sites that are widely publicised as free of charge and sexually liberating are, in fact, little more than shop windows designed to attract and ensnare fee-paying customers. A few dozen free images or videos are usually just the meat on the hook, and a committed pervert will need to hand over his or her credit card details to get full access. Meanwhile amateur net-sex performers are neither uncommercial nor unskilled. The few genuinely free sites I discovered (swinging clubs and couples, compulsive exhibitionists) were heavily linked to commercial sex sites by advertising or by regularly featuring professional net-sex performers. To paraphrase Karl Marx — the internet operates on a no profit, no porn basis.

Many themes continually re-emerge in the study of sex in New Zealand. These include the lurching dichotomy between lust and shame; the wide gap between public ideals and private realities; the feeling that sex is unavoidable and inherently good; that sex is often unwittingly about the hidden power that infuses many social relations — especially the power of money and the power of men. Indeed, the popularity of new wonder drugs like Viagra encapsulates many of these notions. Thousands of impotent men, who previously hid their problem from the cruel light of day, have boldly come out and admitted their failure. Viagra ads depict real blokes, farmers and rough-hewn tradesmen, unashamedly telling how they let their partners down: "Until now I'd kept everything bottled up inside. I couldn't make love to my wife. I was afraid I was going to lose everything. Then I discovered [dramatic pause] … Viagra!"

Though seemingly caring souls, these men evidently share one principal goal — to ejaculate. Most Kiwi males don't believe they have had sex, or at least not good sex, unless they have ejaculated. Viagra erections are therefore a means to getting the male end away. The idea that you are unable to make love without an erect penis is a revealing, but ultimately blinkered outlook. Viagra doesn't seek to enhance sexual performance in its totality — it seeks to make profit from allowing men to ejaculate. A robust test of this thesis would be to manufacture an instant-ejaculation drug — Ejacra? — and distribute it widely and for free. The comparative use and popularity of Ejacra could provide us with a very different picture of heterosexuality and the different roles that men and women are believed to necessarily play. An equivalent female drug — Orgasma? — would be even more enlightening. It isn't difficult to imagine that many women would immediately abandon their routine Friday night drinks-and-grope sessions for a cup of hot cocoa, a torrid romance novel and a small bottle of pink pills. Given our penchant for individualism, the successful manufacture of Ejacra and Orgasma — together with more sophisticated virtual sex — could see us become a country of keyboard romantics, alone at home, secretly smiling in the ghostly glow of our computer screens.

Make a date with these seductive references:

Hawkes G (1996) *A sociology of sex and sexuality,* Philadelphia, Open University Press

Herdt G (ed, 1999) *Sambia sexual culture: essays from the field,* Chicago, University of Chicago Press

Kulick D & M Willson (eds, 1995) *Taboo: sex, identity, and erotic subjectivity in anthropological fieldwork,* London, Routledge

Laumann EO et al (1999) 'Sexual Dysfunction in the United States' *Journal of the American Medical Association,* Vol 281, 6: 537-544 (http://jama.ama.assn.org/issues/v281n6/full/joc80785.html)

Love B (1992) *Encyclopedia of Unusual Sex Practices*, Fort Lee, Barricade Books Inc

Mead M (1943) *Coming of age in Samoa : a study of adolescence and sex in primitive societies*, Harmondsworth, Penguin

Mazengarb O (1954) 'Report of the Special Committee on Moral Delinquency in Children and Adolescents' Wellington, Government Print

Nye RA (1999) *Sexuality*, Oxford University Press

Parker R & P Aggleton (eds, 1999) *Culture, society and sexuality: a reader*, London, UCL Press

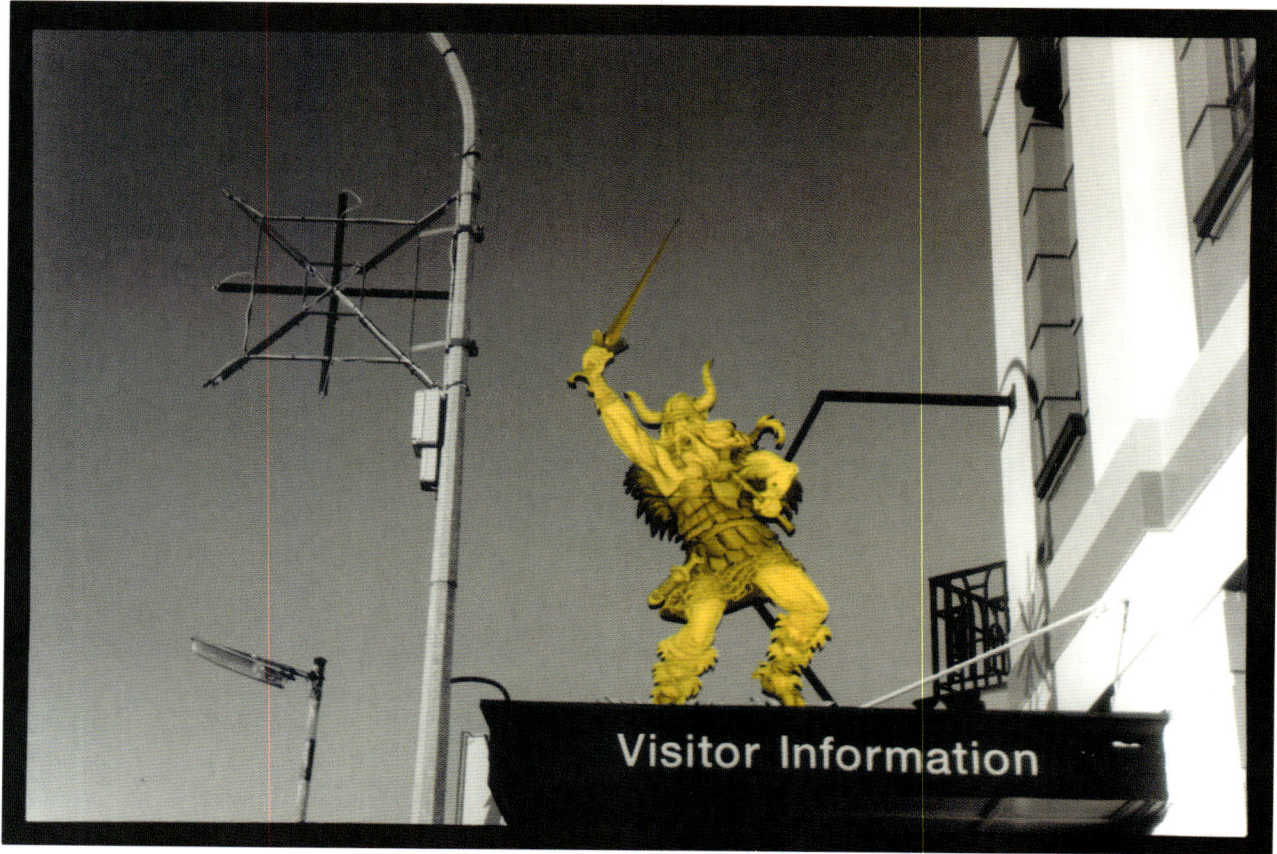

Visitor Information

VI

YOU SAY ETHNICITY, I SAY CULTURE — LET'S CALL THE WHOLE THING …?

IDENTITY, CULTURAL DIFFERENCE & SOCKS

IN THE POST-SLUMBER haze of the early morning, when you find yourself sitting in pyjamas on the side of the bed, do you ever wonder about the cultural, social and identity implications of sock-wearing? Or are you like me, usually distracted by that eternal quest to find a matching pair? I fell into the latter category until one wintry Wellington day in an anthropology tutorial, when discussing the idea that most of our culture is mundane and performed without conscious thought or reflection. Sock/stocking-wearing is but one example of the integral predictability of Kiwi culture. We wear socks with shoes — simple as that. Generally our thinking about sock wearing is confined to the weather, or the work or social event we are about to attend. The more fashion-alert may try and match socks with their clothing, according to current styles, but few of us would be aware of the layers of history, politics, economics and other cultural factors that underlie sock-wearing — indeed which inundate our every act, encounter, utterance and silence. This is because most of culture consists of *doing* rather than *analysing*. If we stopped to minutely inspect the historical and metaphysical implications of our every action — every turn of a tap, every paperclip, every breath or step we take — we would be paralysed, unable to complete even the most banal of activities. Hence the cliché that some dozy academics are out of touch with — and unable to effectively operate in — the real world!

Fortunately we learn most of our culture in ways that are almost unconscious and informal rather than directly taught. Infants often learn by imitating others. As a result, young children may use adult language and mannerisms without any real understanding. My youngest child Estlin had a hearing problem at an early age, so all he could detect were loud sounds. Unfortunately this included my frequent swearing when attempting handyman repairs around the home. So, from a very young age, Estlin would exclaim "Fuck!" as often as other children would say "Mummy." So indiscriminate were his outbursts that we were obliged to tell his grandparents that he was saying "truck" due to his love of all things mechanical.

Without culture we would be nothing more than a mass of biology — eating, sleeping and fornicating in response to instinct. Aside from a few kneejerk responses and the basic physical workings of our bodies, most of what we do is learnt formally and informally and the totality of this learning is our culture. Individuals in distinct cultures will learn quite different things. From opening a door, sitting in a chair or designing a nuclear fusion system, culture is learnt. If the hairs stand up on the back of your neck when the All Blacks do a haka — or you gagged when you heard Paul Holmes' CD — this shows a learnt Kiwi culture. Someone from another culture — say one of the intergalactic characters from the TV comedy *Third Rock from the Sun* — may have no concept of a door, a chair or nuclear energy. They could see the All Black's haka as little more than an incoherent cacophony of noise and flailing limbs — to say nothing of Holmes' singing. Some anthropological studies conclude that apparently natural phenomena, such as the colours that people see, may also be determined by their culture. The Hanunóo of the Philippines use a colour system that focuses on whether objects are wet, lush or dry. The Hanunóo simply do not have colours, in terms of different pigments, hues or tints, as we would understand them.

The culture of adults consists of categories of understanding (what is thought of as an animal, a plant, etc) which allow us to communicate meaningfully through language, symbols and acts. Yet whenever I ask people what is characteristic of New Zealand culture they tend to concentrate on things they think are unique and distinctive (gumboots, the kiwi, Fiordland) — or on high culture (the music of the Finn brothers, the scribblings of Katherine Mansfield, the haka). While these are definitely part of our culture, they are more typical of the idealism and romanticism found in a Tourism New Zealand campaign than our everyday lives in all their massed, inglorious routine. So while our culture definitely includes rugby, Maori customs, the poems of James K Baxter and the operatic warblings of Kiri Te Kanawa, it also consists of the million small things we habitually do with little thought or reflection. This includes queuing for fish'n'chips, drinking from a glass, using an ATM, catching taxis in the rain, wearing underpants and watching American sitcoms on TV.

Culture is continuously learnt and re-learnt from the cradle to the grave. This is partly because all cultures are constantly transformed through technological advances, contact with other cultures, demographic changes and the like. A hundred years ago most people would have been able to tell the difference between a sloop and a ketch moored in Wellington Harbour. Today we are more likely to be able to distinguish between a Toyota and a Porsche zooming down Ngauranga Gorge. And although it may appear that cultures come and go, no person is ever bereft of culture — people always have culture. This apparent paradox exists because culture resides in the experiences, knowledge and actions of individuals. In other words, you and I *are* New Zealand culture. So while Nike cross-trainers may have replaced the Skellerup gumboot as footwear for the outdoors — and people predictably lament the loss of Kiwi culture — it is not really lost at all, but merely transformed. Similarly, you often hear people lamenting the loss of this culture or that, of the demise of ancient Greek or authentic Maori culture. But as culture resides in each person's ever-changing understandings and practices, culture *per se* can never be lost. Specific cultural elements can be transformed, replaced or re-labelled, but culture of one form or another will always be found

> *A hundred years ago most people would have been able to tell the difference between a sloop and a ketch moored in Wellington Harbour. Today we are more likely to be able to distinguish between a Toyota and a Porsche zooming down Ngauranga Gorge.*

wherever humans and rats (that's another story) hang out. Culture is also rarely bound by time or space — it travels with every New Zealander on their O.E. and likewise is open to every overseas influence capable of gaining a toehold. Tikka masala is much a part of our culture as it is a part of the culture of India … Sydney, New York, London …

We also constantly re-learn our culture as our own roles in society change. My journey from youth to parent was marked when I no longer gagged in the presence of someone vomiting. I used to think that gagging was an instinctive, involuntary response. But I have been convinced otherwise by my children and their kaleidoscopic responses to too many sweets, changes in the seasons and the Rimutaka hill road. In raising children, my knowledge and experiences — i.e. my culture — have altered. My children's vomit has become something to catch, clean up and even inspect to diagnose the cause of their illnesses. Student nurses report similar changes. The sights, sounds and smells of sickness that initially offended their sensibilities become part of their caring repertoire. Student nurses quickly learn to identify the different emissions of the ailing, to work out the response required.

You may not have enjoyed the giddy delights of the non-gagging response, but this does not mean that we don't share a culture. If you can read this essay, then we share a culture no matter what our skin colour, gender, ethnic identity, class or whatever. At a minimum, we share in the categorical knowledge of writing; we understand that the essay is to be read, that the language used is English and that it appears on a page. Whether you agree with the arguments I present is quite a different question. To be members of a shared culture does not mean that we have exactly the same knowledge, attitudes, values or opinions. In fact, it is only within a shared culture that individuals can have a meaningful disagreement. I once arrived at the Portuguese-Spanish frontier, only to be confronted by an upset border guard. At least I assume he was upset, as I didn't speak Spanish or he English — to my ears his spluttering and gnashing speech was simply noise without meaning. Neither was I familiar with how Spaniards express feelings. For all I knew his wild gesticulations could have indicated he wished to propose marriage. As we did not share a language or the core categories of meaning that make up a culture, we could not communicate much. However, we did agree that he was a border guard and that I was a foreign tourist and when he took his revolver from its holster the mutual understandings of authority and power quickly came to the fore. I hurriedly shoved every conceivable travel document in front of him. Apparently pacified, he curtly waved me away — I hadn't been such a good marriage prospect after all.

Such gross cultural differences do not allow for a deep understanding of each other, or even a shared misunderstanding. We observe, interpret and describe others through the lens of our own culture. When some of the highland tribes of Papua New Guinea first saw Europeans — the three Leahy brothers of Australia who led an expedition to find gold in 1930 — they believed they were their ancestors returned from the dead. As the highlanders wore little more than a few leaves covering the genital area, they thought that the Europeans wore long trousers to hide their enormous penises. Nothing had prepared them for white-skinned people, and their initial impressions were based on their existing cultural categories. After this first contact, however, the cultures of both groups were transformed and the highlanders quickly adjusted to the Europeans. As one highlander commented: "Their shit smells just like ours." This type of circumstance makes New Zealand's own bi- and multi-culturalism seem rather tame. Much of the debate on relations between the so-called 'different cultures' in New Zealand is actually premised on the fact that the groups share enough culture to enable meaningful dialogue. Ironically, as the culture of McDonald's and Coca-Cola relentlessly dominate the globe and we all become ever more alike, the more able we are to meaningfully share and exalt our differences. A Maori arts administrator recently expressed his new-found appreciation for the English language because it had enabled Maori artists to communicate their cultural ideas to Canadian Indians who also spoke English.

This emergent transglobal culture of common language, beliefs, values, social customs, categories of meaning, political and economic structures, desire, symbols, etc, raises the issue of just how different today's cultures are from one another. How different is New Zealand culture from that of Australia, Britain, the US and Canada? Is our culture — as so many politicians, tourism executives and other commentators proclaim — unique? One answer is that New Zealand culture is unique because we have languages, art forms, customs, beliefs and practices not found elsewhere in the world to any significant degree. We have unique languages — Maori and New Zealand English — that may be uttered in Sydney, London and elsewhere, but are predominantly spoken in Aotearoa and mostly in homegrown settings (e.g. the marae, at Eden Park test matches). We also have unique foods (the pavlova, huhu grubs, Pacific fusion cooking, kina) that may grace the tables of restaurants around the globe, but which allegedly originated in New Zealand and are not found to the same extent elsewhere. We have unique values (the tangata whenua's spiritual link with Aotearoa, our love of rugby and our long-time pursuit of egalitarianism). We have unique customs (the All Black haka, wearing jandals to work) and so on. And if our culture does include McDonald's and Coca-Cola, then they are manufactured and consumed in ways unique to us (e.g. the McKiwi burger).

Yet cultural uniqueness is not difficult to achieve. Any form of uniqueness needs only one aspect of difference between two entities. To say that our culture is unique compared to that of Australia simply requires that Aussies drink beer from tinnies while we sup from cans, no matter that both are cylindrical objects made of aluminium and specifically designed to hold fizzy beverages. In this respect New Zealand culture is unique in much the same way that every person, plant, animal and rock is unique — at least before the advent of genetic cloning and the Green Party. If we also accept that no human activity is ever exactly duplicated, that there is no precise replication of Kiwi culture over time, then we begin to realise that all cultures throughout history and around the globe are by definition unique. The more pertinent question is, therefore: is New Zealand culture *significantly* distinct from others?

We may claim that New Zealand culture has distinctive elements (e.g. te reo Maori), but at the same time recognise that it also shares much (market economy, democratic central government, K-Mart, air pollution, etc) with other cultures, such as our predominantly English-speaking cousins — the Australians, Canadians, British and Americans. Yet distinctiveness is no guarantee of social value. For example, we could list everything that is Kiwi culture — every material object, social encounter, meaning category, symbol, political philosophy. We might rank items by:

- The number of social situations in which they occur
- How many people perform or reproduce them
- The influence they exert in people's thoughts, beliefs, values, acts and interactions.

Such an exercise would produce a very different picture of New Zealand culture. We might conclude that elements such as Maori language and our passion for rugby — although distinctive and held in high regard by many — have limited social currency, especially when compared to other more mundane and far less esteemed things, such as eating toast or driving cars. For example, Maori language enjoys its greatest social influence on the marae, in Kohanga Reo learning nests, in Maori-speaking households and on Maori TV. Whatever you feel about te reo Maori, and regardless of change in the future, it is simply not the daily language of most Kiwis.

The 2001 census revealed that of the approximately half a million people identified as Maori, 494,679 (95%) speak English and 130,482 (25%) speak Maori. And most of us would be hard-pressed to correctly guess the third and fourth most popular languages among Maori. 'None' (i.e. too young to talk) ranked third with 17,376 non-speakers (or 'gurglers' as they are technically called) and New Zealand Sign Language rated fourth with 6,549 participants. According to our criteria Maori language is less socially vital (at least in terms of discourse) than English, which is the language of daily thought, talk and business for most Pakeha and Maori. And while the English we speak can be characterised as New Zealand English — unique in that we say fush'n'chups and often use Maori terms (almost everyone seems to have a whanau these days) — it is vastly more like Australian English, American English and English English, than it is different.

Our reputed passion for rugby is also socially limited to the settings of the rugby ground, public bars or pay-to-view Sky TV. A similar passion for rugby can be found in Wales, South Africa and the richer areas of England. Moreover, this passion is very like that felt by many Americans for baseball and gridiron, Canadians for ice hockey and Victorian Aussies for Rules. Our apparently unique love of rugby also overlooks the fact that a minority of New Zealanders actively play, coach or administer the game. According to Hillary Commission (now SPARC) statistics, 137,100 adults actively took part in rugby in 2000. Of course many thousands more regularly watch or are interested in it, yet golf had some 332,500 players and women's netball 154,900. Somewhat surprisingly, recreational walking was the most popular leisure activity, attracting 746,260 regular strollers. It is also sobering to note that the New Zealand Rugby Union boasted only 98,543 paid-up members in 2000 — compared with New Zealand Soccer which had 105,023 and Netball New Zealand 120,440. All these figures pale when compared with the millions of us who regularly partake in that most popular of leisure activities — shopping. We might conclude that shopping outweighs rugby as a marker of Kiwi culture. And this is the same type of shopping that — when you have the financial resources — can be conducted just as easily at Kirkcaldies (Wellington) as it can at David Jones (Melbourne), Harrods (London), Macy's (New York) or anywhere in the world, given appropriate internet facilitates and a credit card.

In developing this idea we move towards the conclusion that the most socially significant aspects of Kiwi culture are the most common things. This includes wearing pyjamas, opening and closing doors, having hot and cold tapped water, buying a daily paper, eating chocolate bars, doing everyday work. These activities are remarkably like those that also characterise the cultures of Australia, USA, Singapore and South Africa. The litmus test of our culture's distinctiveness is whether your average, competent Kiwi can function in a 'different' culture. Leaving aside the issues of passport, visa and residency rules of different countries, the test is whether you can communicate, eat, sleep, find shelter, gain sexual jollies, get work, understand political processes and so on in a 'different' culture and within the range of effectiveness routinely enjoyed by the resident people. If the answer is yes, we may conclude that the cultures are more similar than different. Indeed, as previously distinctive cultures around the world gradually succumb to globalisation, even greater numbers of globe-trotting Kiwis will be able to effectively and competently live away from the Land of the Long White Cloud (see Chapter 7). Where then will the boundaries of New Zealand culture be drawn?

But I digress from my discussion of socks and the midwinter anthro tutorial. I was casting around for an example of the mundane, unreflective 'doing' of culture, when it occurred to me that one of my students never wore footwear. On this day the rest of the student group was garbed in long scarves, puffy jackets and stout shoes — including the apparently obligatory socks. I asked who had given reflective thought to wearing socks that day, but most had simply worn them: "It's what you do." This led to

… they thought that the Europeans wore long trousers to hide their enormous penises.

a discussion about the cultural and social ethos of sock wearing. The presence or absence of socks can define context, time and morality. As expected, most of us generally wear socks in formal and public contexts (at work, shopping); their absence can denote informal (at the beach) or more private (in bed) circumstances. Middle-class people often comment unfavourably on parents whose children go barefoot in public or in bad weather. Such judgements reveal the class dimensions and social disciplines of sock wearing, although they do not necessarily apply in rural areas where it is common to see schoolkids walking home without shoes or socks, even in winter. If the weather is fine, then barefoot children, whether urban or rural, are simply seen as evidence of the carefree days of summer. Ethnicity further complicates this picture as many Kiwis think that being barefoot is 'normal' for individuals from different cultures (e.g. Pacific Islanders).

From this brief foray it may be seen that sock wearing is richly layered with social, moral and cultural influences — most of which we unconsciously and habitually reproduce on a daily basis. In contrast, the barefoot student in our tutorial was highly aware that his non-wearing of socks and shoes was a potent statement of difference: "My bare feet are a sign that I act and think differently from the common herd." This student had consciously chosen to highlight his uniqueness through a public symbol that was markedly different from the norm. In this he joined a long list of luminaries from Jesus Christ to Mahatma Gandhi and James K Baxter, who all went barefoot to demonstrate that they were opposed to the status quo. In fact, all identities are constructed and expressed in comparison with others (male/female; fat/thin; Maori/Pakeha). As such, most overt expressions of identity are designed to exclude others as much as to mark fellow birds of a feather. Yet what is overlooked in the analysis of identities is often the most obvious — they are conscious and articulate, while the largest chunk of culture is unconscious and inarticulate. Though all identities are part of culture, not all culture is necessarily incorporated within identities. That's why, for most of us, although sock/stocking wearing is part of our daily lives, it's not part of how we choose to identify ourselves. Tourism campaigns depict exotic (to the tourist) aspects of our culture — Maori in traditional piupiu, farmers in black singlets and gumboots; but nowhere is the humble Hallenstein's sock to be seen (the famous lucky red socks of Team New Zealand's various America's Cup campaigns notwithstanding).

This point is especially germane when considering ethnic identities, which many revealingly think of as synonymous with culture. Pakeha ethnicity as an identity has gained support recently with the advent of the First Ships of 1850 celebrations in Christchurch and such books as *Being Pakeha* by Michael King. That the emergence of a Pakeha ethnicity postdates the clarion call for Maori sovereignty by the proto-radical Donna

Awatere in early 1980s is no coincidence. As Maori have sought to cast aside European imperialism they have expressed a highly conscious identity. This identity often embodies calls for self-determination as many Maori proclaim their special status as tangata whenua (i.e. indigenous, first-nation people) of Aotearoa/New Zealand. Such claims contain direct and implicit comparisons with non-Maori — especially with the descendants of European settlers and more recent immigrants who are collectively referred to as Pakeha. At the extremes, Maori are seen as somehow having a more authentic culture, expressed in an innate spiritual union with the land and in kinship-based relationships. Conversely, Pakeha are cast as an individualistic rabble, driven by greed, with no real affinity to the land, and therefore devoid of real culture and spirituality.

This has compelled a plethora of Pakeha literati, academics, social commentators and regional élite to express their own versions of ethnicity or culture — versions which clearly parallel those of Maori while also attempting to highlight points of difference. Many have commented that being Pakeha involves an active acknowledgment and redress of the injustices visited on Maori. Others have noted that like Maori, Pakeha:

- Have a collective name
- Share a common myth of descent and history (i.e. from Abel Tasman onwards)
- Link with a specific territory (more than 90% of Pakeha today were born in New Zealand)
- Have a sense of solidarity that emerged as ties to Mother

England were gradually severed after World War II and the UK joined the European Economic Community in 1973

- Share a distinctive culture that consists of rugby, Lotto and sauvignon blanc; a love of New Zealand's clean, green spaces; the pioneer, No. 8 wire spirit; a commitment to the principles of egalitarianism, and so on.

Many commentators slip between discussing Pakeha ethnicity and Pakeha culture without missing a beat. For them, culture and ethnicity are one and the same thing. Yet what is missing from these eloquent expressions are the million everyday things that actually form the core of culture in New Zealand — a core that is daily experienced by Pakeha and Maori alike. Promoters of Pakeha ethnicity never proudly proclaim: "I eat potatoes, drink water and defecate in a toilet. My trousers have pockets in which there is a $1 coin and some tissue paper. I am Pakeha. I am unique!" Claims of ethnic difference are affirmative statements of the exotic, the ideal, the romantic or the desired. They also border on the illusory. Pakeha's apparent affinity with the New Zealand wilderness belies the fact that more than 85% of us are committed urbanites who wouldn't know a totara from a rimu. Furthermore, the ethos of Kiwi ingenuity overlooks the reality that most Pakeha are paper-pushers who could no more swing a hammer than they could fell a tree, and that No. 8 wire is no longer manufactured anyway. In this light we have

Pakeha's apparent affinity with the wilderness belies the fact that more than 85% of them are committed urbanites who wouldn't know a totara from a rimu.

to consider whether the claims of Pakeha ethnicity are rhetorical — little more than idealised hot air, and with even less social import.

We are constantly encouraged by educators, advertisers and life coaches to find and express our authentic selves — personal, sexual, ethnic, national and so on. Sometimes what is branded authentic is more likely to be idealised. Yet what authentic Pakeha ethnicity predominantly involves is watching TV, using perforated toilet paper and perceiving that the sky is blue and that rain is wet. But then again so does authentic Maori ethnicity and so does authentic Kiwi culture. This summons to express our authentic and unique identities is largely connected with the democratic right of individuals to choose freely between different life pathways and to express themselves without fear. But expressions of identity are also linked to subtle — and not so subtle — power-plays between different socio-political groups. Many who took part in the conflicts in Rwanda, the former Yugoslavia and elsewhere were given a political free-card to truly express their ethnicity. The result was total inhumanity towards those who did not fit the prescribed ethnic, cultural or 'racial' characteristics. So where do the trustworthy boundaries of ethnicity and culture lie?

The more cynical of us can plot a direct link between the desire to express distinctive identities and the economic demands of consumerism, which are also based on the endless quest for variety. From clothing fashions to the latest in IT technology and the re-emergence of Classic Coke, scooters and retro-music, the perpetual desire for the trendy and exotic are cornerstones of modern commerce. This world of difference also tends to exist at the level of ideas, rhetoric and aesthetics, rather than in basic social structures and practices. The popularity of Trade Aid shops is a case in point. The desire to support disenfranchised Third World peoples by buying their arts and crafts appears laudable. Yet the artefacts on display are removed from the original symbolic, cultural and social worlds in which they were produced — effectively reduced to mere emblems of ethnic difference and of the liberal middle classes' concern for the less privileged in faraway places. They are also turned into commodities — little different from a bottle of milk — produced, distributed and sold for profit. No profit, no production, no Trade Aid shop. The manufacture of such artefacts on what is in effect a capitalist model actually compels Third World peoples to be further integrated into the global market. When this occurs people tend to lose their indigenous cultures and become homeogenised units in a mass economy.

To express your authentic or ideal identity is an economic and political freedom enjoyed by few, denied to many. It assumes disposable resources, skills, knowledge and money that may be channelled into the conscious symbolism of identity difference. The bigger the bucks, the greater the potential to fully express yourself. The world's 200 richest people, with a combined wealth of US$ one trillion (a thousand billion), are clearly capable of expressing themselves from the stockmarkets of New York to the casinos of Monte Carlo. Can you imagine Donald Trump being too tongue-tied or socially gagged to articulate the many layers of his complex, enthralling self? It's a different story for the 600 million inhabitants of the world's 43 least-developed countries, who share a combined income of only US$145 billion. For the most part, physical survival consumes their daily lives. The expression of their transglobal identities — as Third World peoples — is mostly left to a host of First World others ranging from aid agencies to CNN News. Meanwhile, freedom of self-expression is completely denied every day to the 30,000 children who die, malnourished and deprived. In their brief lives they were unable to learn any of the machinations of identity expression, cultural difference or ethnicity. They were unable to learn, enact or interact at all. The issue then, is what can we learn from them? Ka ora tonu ra te mauri o te iwi Pakeha ia ra ia ra?

Go ahead, express yourself … choose one of the following:

Connolly B & R Anderson (1987) *First Contact: New Guinea's highlanders encounter the outside world*, New York, Viking Books, also available in video format (1982), Canberra, Ronin Films

www.funbureau.com/ The Bureau of Missing Socks

Goodenough W (1994) 'Toward a Working Theory of Culture' in R Borofsky (ed), *Assessing Cultural Anthropology*, New York, McGraw-Hill

Harrison S (1999) 'Cultural Boundaries' *Anthropology Today*, 15 (5):10-13

www.sparc.org.nz: site for Sport & Recreation New Zealand

Hobsbawm E & T Ranger (1996) *The Invention of Tradition*, Cambridge University Press

King M (1985) *Being Pakeha: an encounter with Maori renaissance*, Auckland, Hodder & Stoughton

King M (ed, 1991) *Pakeha: A Quest for Identity in New Zealand*, Auckland, Penguin Books

Nash R (1990) 'Society and Culture in New Zealand: an outburst for 1990' *New Zealand Sociology*, 5 (2): 99-124

Wright S (1998) 'The Politicization of Culture,' *Anthropology Today*, 14 (1): 7-15

Pearson D (1989) 'Pakeha Ethnicity: Concept or Conundrum' *Sites*, 18: 61-72

Smith AD (1986) *The Ethnic Origins of Nations*, Cambridge University Press

www.undp.org/hdro/ United Nations Development Programme: Human Development Report

Urry J (1995) 'Ethnicizing the World', unpublished paper presented to the NZASA conference, Wellington, available from the Anthropology Department, Victoria University of Wellington

Watson JL (1997) *Golden Arches East: McDonald's in East Asia*, California, Stanford University Press

VII

WHITE CROSSES ON THE ROADSIDE: NON-PLACES AND NON-PEOPLE

PLACE, PERSONHOOD, ECONOMICS & MOBILITY

WHEN YOU TRAVEL the decrepit highways and byways that pass for our roading system you can hardly fail to notice the plaintive white crosses that speckle the roadside. Nailed to fenceposts or planted askew on the verge, they are often adorned with artificial flowers and brief details — *Steve, aged 19; Lorraine, 1981-1998*. As simple expressions of loss they are timely warnings of the fragility of life in the fast lane.

The first crosses were put up in 1990 by concerned citizens of Katikati to highlight the hazards of a local stretch of State Highway 2. After gaining the support of people who had lost family members in the area, the group planted 53 crosses over two weekends. Transit New Zealand immediately objected that the crosses were a distraction to motorists and pulled them out. Over the next few weeks the crosses were re-erected, then taken down by Transit, then re-erected … and so on.

By 1993 the crosses were an iconic feature of all New Zealand's roadways and had even been incorporated into Transit New Zealand's formal road-safety policy "to show where fatal accidents had occurred and to serve as a road-safety reminder."

Leaving aside the obvious Christian symbolism, the crosses are also potent metaphors of a recent and fundamental social change, especially for the middle classes who daily cruise past them and whose lives are distinguished by mobility in all facets. For the places where these white crosses stand, where lives young and old were brutally terminated, are non-places, neither here nor there, *liminal* places — anonymous passageways between home and elsewhere. The non-place is the opposite of your family home, workplace or local sports club. Familiar places are where you are an acknowledged personality, an established or much loved character who shares your life with others and who has well-known moralities, beliefs, ideologies, talents and skills. In that place you are a lover, a parent, an aunt, a colleague, a friend … a named entity. By contrast, in the non-place few know your name, fewer still even care. The structure of the non-place decrees that the richness and depth of a person — their loves, hates, experiences and values — are muted or are of little moment. Although the victims of roadside accidents may warrant biographical snippets in the daily news, their deaths quickly become opportunities for experts to attribute statistical blame and before the year's end will be subsumed within the road toll — traffic fatalities #120, #121 …

The non-place can also be found in airport terminals, shopping malls, high-rise hotels, fast-food joints and mass-leisure sites like movie theatres and rugby stadiums. Although these are among our most significant sites of collective and face-to-face social encounter, the non-place effectively devours our individuality. We pass fleetingly through it, stopping only briefly to eat, sleep or do business. In the non-place we take — but rarely make — friends. We are too busy, time-poor, always on the go. In the non-place we move far too fast to stop and embrace humanity. This is despite mobile phones that enable us to constantly track the movements of our friends and thereby locate ourselves. In the non-place we are set adrift in a sea of uncaring and mercenary others. We are classified (and we constantly classify others) into categories. Personalised humanity is lost among myriad groupings of class, gender, age, brand of clothing, or whether we have the right forms of ID to enable entry or credit-card processing. In the non-place the individual is essentially cast as a non-person.

Society in New Zealand, especially among urban or city folk, is increasingly full of non-people. This is partly due to the dynamics of population growth — there are simply too many individuals to know on an intimate basis. But it is also influenced by the fact that we are increasingly unfixed in our lifetime endeavours. The middle classes in particular change career, home, class and even life partners with startling rapidity as we constantly seek to improve our lot in life. Short-term social relationships are ever more likely to be the norm. Demographic explosions and individual mobility combine to ensure that inter-actions with others are transient and less personal. That our friends or family think of us as a good or lousy lover, a caring or neglectful parent, a brave or fearful survivor of cancer is of little relevance to thousands of unknowable others who also regularly inhabit non-places.

There are others, though — such as vendors, marketers and advertisers — who are far more calculating. Your recent warm embrace of your child is quickly aligned with their assessment of your credit-card capacity and predicted spending patterns. Advertisers may strive to convince you that a child's love should be rewarded with a store-bought gift, but don't kid yourself that they really care. To them you are little more than a market category — male, Pakeha, aged 40-49, divorced, earning $75,000, tertiary educated and packing a gold Amex. Once you are marked and tagged, all strings are pulled to ensure maximal profit flows from your most personal feelings. The common desire among divorcees to overcompensate by showering their children with gifts and overseas trips may be psychologically suspect, but it is also a marketer's dream. We may feel and think as individuals, and those who really love us — our friends and family — positively nurture our distinct awareness of self, but these homespun cocoons of individuality blind us to our categorised and commodified anonymity within the non-place.

Yet daily we use these same categories and classifications to express our own sense of self. For example, the renaissance of ethnic identity — especially contemporary Maori and Pakeha — is partly due to the host of bureaucratic and other groups that constantly demand we declare this form of personhood. From applying for an IRD number to university enrolment, ethnic identification is a must-have. You may have given little serious thought to whether ethnicity exerts a big influence in your everyday life, but when confronted by an institutional stalwart who can approve or dismiss our claim for a government benefit, most of us will comply by choosing an ethnic identity from the range offered. Our choice is determined by the range the institution has deemed appropriate. Individuals participating in the 1996 census had the option of declaring themselves to be New Zealand European or Pakeha. Yet according to Statistics New Zealand, the Pakeha dimension had disappeared five years later and all that was left in the 2001 census was the New Zealand European component. The department claimed it was only responding to social trends in removing Pakeha as an ethnic option. Apparently individuals had complained on a variety of grounds, including that they felt 'Pakeha' was a derogatory term for white New Zealanders. Those who had only just become comfortable with *Being Pakeha* found their new ethnicity had been consigned to the trashcan of failed identities with one flourish of a bureaucrat's pen.

As we become more mobile and increasingly exist as non-people, we ironically heighten our awareness of what makes us distinct from others, others from others, and our current from our past selves — though Shirley Maclaine's well-known reincarnations are an exception to this rule. In other words, we gain an enhanced ability to express our distinctive individual identity. As we move from job to job, lover to lover, place to place we have to regularly re-invent ourselves — to adopt new roles, improve our personae and generate new alibis. This endless differentiating of the self — this cult of individuality — has become highly valued in our society and is further fuelled by marketing gurus who promise self-realisation in a bottle of Pantene or CK *One*. In this respect, individual mobility and blended families are two sides of the same coin — constant change impairs our ability to make lasting social bonds, hence the increased turnover of friends, lovers and one-bedroom apartments. And the economic benefits are unbelievable! The resulting individuality represents the ultimate in consumerism as each of us buys our own house, lounge suite and lawnmower.

Yet in another paradox, our constant mobility and change are actually caused by us being more alike and less different. Prior to the 15th century the ancestors of many Pakeha lived in distinct settlements spread throughout Britain and Europe. These disparate communities often had their own languages, numeracy, religions, social and cultural systems. Individuals from different communities, sometimes separated by less than a crow's flight, could be very different in speech and custom. People were basically immobile — they were geographically, socially and culturally static. They lived and died in the communities of their birth or marriage.

Since the 15th century, and especially since the industrial revolution, money or capital has become ever more mobile in its search for markets. By the end of the second millennium the volume of financial dealings on global currency markets had topped a trillion US dollars per day. And wherever capital goes, the labour force follows. By the late 18th century the need for workers was exponential as new industries rapidly spread throughout Europe and else-where. From the rural outposts of Britain to the heartlands of Africa and the tropical beaches of the Pacific, labour was extracted like ore and thrown together in a global melting pot. Today this process is even more highly evolved. In 2000 more than 375,000 New Zealand-born individuals were living across the ditch in Australia — likewise the 2001 census revealed that nearly 23% (846,411) of our resident population was born overseas.

Who serves you at McDonald's, performs your gynaecological probes or collects your rubbish — friend, family or stranger?

The profitable movement of peoples, drawn from very different cultural backgrounds to create a global labour market, was partly achieved by ensuring they were eventually integrated in a collective culture, speaking the same language and sharing a numerical system. For example, previously distinct com-munities throughout Britain had localised solar time. Around the end of the 18th century local mean time was kept by clocks, but it still differed between communities. As rail systems grew to service the industrial revolution, local times were replaced by British Standard Time in the mid-19th century to enable reliable rail connections. Similarly New Zealand adopted its own standard time in 1868, even though the colony could only boast 40 or so miles of public railway — although by 1879 we had more than 1100 miles of railway thanks to Julius Vogel and his great public works programme. In 1884 Greenwich Mean Time was adopted by all the major developing nations, enabling them to effectively compare their different time zones. In terms of a shared language, we need only note that to this day English remains the dominant global language of business, science, aviation, and many other activities with more than 1.5 billion speakers worldwide. Once people share a language and do sums the same way it is a relatively easy matter to redeploy them wherever new markets emerge or to re-educate them in new manufacturing techniques. It is also comparatively simple to sell them a consistent diet of Coca-Cola, McDonald's and New Zealand cheese in places as far apart as Taupo and Dubai.

Unlike our ancestors, most Kiwis today are not bound by the localism of place, people or social circumstance. In our lifetime we may have a succession of careers in various parts of the world. We may leave behind the class, religion and philosophies of our parents, family and friends to re-invent ourselves time and again.

I first realised that I had transcended the class of my birth when my fantasies about women who rode motorbikes were replaced by those of women who played the violin. I now find myself easily bored with a full game of rugby and generally keep my inheritance alive by watching edited highlights on TV. Actually, a brief analysis of rugby neatly reveals the increased mobility and institutionalisation of our social existence. Back a generation or two most players spent their entire rugby careers playing for the communities of their birth or, if they were hot stuff, for their region or nation. In many cases once their international careers were over they returned to play for, coach or administer their local teams. The great Pinetree Meads was born in Te Kuiti and played for the local primary, college and club teams before being selected in the regional King Country squad. After a distinguished All Black career he returned to coach King Country and served local and national rugby in a variety of managerial positions. So did his brother Stan.

Players today face altogether new propositions and many play for several different clubs, regions or even sporting codes — sometimes within one season. In the Super 12, regional ties are nominal, while players in the draft pool may play for more than one franchise in a season. Those who were team-mates throughout the Super 12 are just as likely to be opponents in the NPC season later the same year. Players can also swap to rugby

As rugby has become run on a business ethos … players are now commodities that can be bought and sold on the open market

league and back again with relative ease. Marc Ellis played for Wellington College, Otago University, Otago Highlanders, the All Blacks, the Auckland Warriors, the Kiwi rugby league team, North Harbour and the Auckland Blues. Some even change the country they represent — as the number of former Kiwis playing in Japan and Europe testifies. The Leslie brothers, John and Martin, may have been raised in the cold winds of the Petone recreation ground, but their playing careers stretch from Wellington to Dunedin to Scotland — and they haven't finished yet.

These days the main obstacle to the mobility of individual rugby players is contractual — have the right conditions been met, has the right amount of money changed hands? As rugby is now run on a business model it has inevitably succumbed to the demands of mobile capital. Players are now commodities to be bought and sold on the market — hence the will-he-won't-he dramas that surrounded Jonah Lomu whenever his contract with the New Zealand Rugby Union came up for renewal. It is also notable that recent All Black teams have contained very few from rural backgrounds. In Pinetree Meads' time, the bulk of forwards were dredged from family farms. They were often giant, taciturn men who showed a commitment to the Silver Fern that was only surpassed by their loyalty to the farms and places of their forefathers. As rugby has gradually become a middle-class job, the mobility of players has increased. This — combined with the global transferability of knowledge and skills, the centralisation of commerce and power in affluent urban places and the correlated decrease in the number of individuals bound to the land and community — has robbed the All Black pack of rough-hewn farmers and some much-needed mongrel.

The evolution of world markets, together with the growth of a culturally compatible global workforce, has resulted in heavily populated societies that stretch from Wellington to London to New York. The rise of the non-place is to be expected, as millions of strangers are obliged to interact with each other on a daily basis. Much of our life is now dominated by encounters with strangers — from automated telephone voices and complete strangers on the bus, to comparative strangers at work. Many of us are obviously still surrounded by family and friends — especially in certain social settings (e.g. the home) and at certain stages of our life-cycle (e.g. when the kids are young). But think about how many of your family work together? How many still live in the same town or even in the same country? Who serves you at McDonald's, performs your gynaecological probes or collects your rubbish — friend, family or stranger? Today our social ties with each other are more likely to be mediated by the Consumer Guarantees Act than they are by enduring biographical knowledge and personal warmth.

Strangers in non-places may actually interact more effectively without any in-depth, personal attachment and through a series of socially scripted, formulaic and relatively predictable acts.

Although customised dialogue is engaged whenever we buy goods — from the "Hello, can I help you" to "Would you like fries with that?" — few words actually need pass between retailer and consumer, as the relationship is largely contractual and this ritual is learned in early childhood. Indeed, I often feel uncomfortable when a shop assistant or petrol-pump attendant engages me in friendly banter by asking me how life is treating me or by proffering an innocuous opinion on the day's leading news story. Although I know that this chit-chat is scripted by corporate overseers to enhance customer relations, I feel uncertain how to reply to what initially appears as a personable invitation to meaningful dialogue. My instinct is to respond honestly as a slightly-crazed, neo-marxist anthropologist with two kids, a loving partner and an ever-growing student loan. But replying in this manner always seems to cut the chat dead, so I've recently taken to grunting uncivilly. In a similar scenario, I once witnessed someone respond to the shop assistant by revealing that they had just been diagnosed with secondary breast cancer and were extremely fearful of their future prospects. The assistant's response was a flustered: "Well, I'll get this wrapped straight away then." In essence the non-place reduces individuals to the level of a sign (customer) and enables them to associate with others as signs (customer: shopkeeper) via a series of pre-scripted lines that enable complete strangers to engage in mutually beneficial exchange. A clutter of signs — from price tags to credit cards — are all that's needed to enable non-people to trade.

Many of us find formulaic social intercourse barren and lacking real connection. My research has shown that many of those who journey to the boutique wine village of Martinborough in the Wairarapa seek interactions that go beyond the merely contractual. These predominantly Wellingtonian tourists want to get to know the winemakers, homestay operators and local craftspeople — to learn something of the personal histories and philosophies which underpin their products. In this respect many of the tourists harbour nostalgic visions of a mythical Golden Past when rural folk toiled long and honestly, skilfully nurturing the fruits of Mother Nature, all the while working side-by-side with generations of family and friends. The tourists' distaste for the sterile and prescribed activities common in their urban lives is nevertheless limited. Their interest in the locals is mostly confined to either the feel-good factors of consumerism or to trying to snag a bargain off the simple rural folk. Many love to hear winemakers describe their noble quests to produce the perfect pinot noir, but their minds wander at the first mention of hefty mortgages, the hard physical work and the negative economies of running small-scale vineyards. When jaded Kiwi urbanites venture into rural spaces the sun literally blinds them to the real lie of the land.

There is, however, an element of reality in the tourists' delusions. Most rural places have a core of inhabitants who, by virtue of being generationally bound to the land, are relatively immobile or static. Many rural people share the knowledge and experience of each other's first pair of gumboots, their hooning

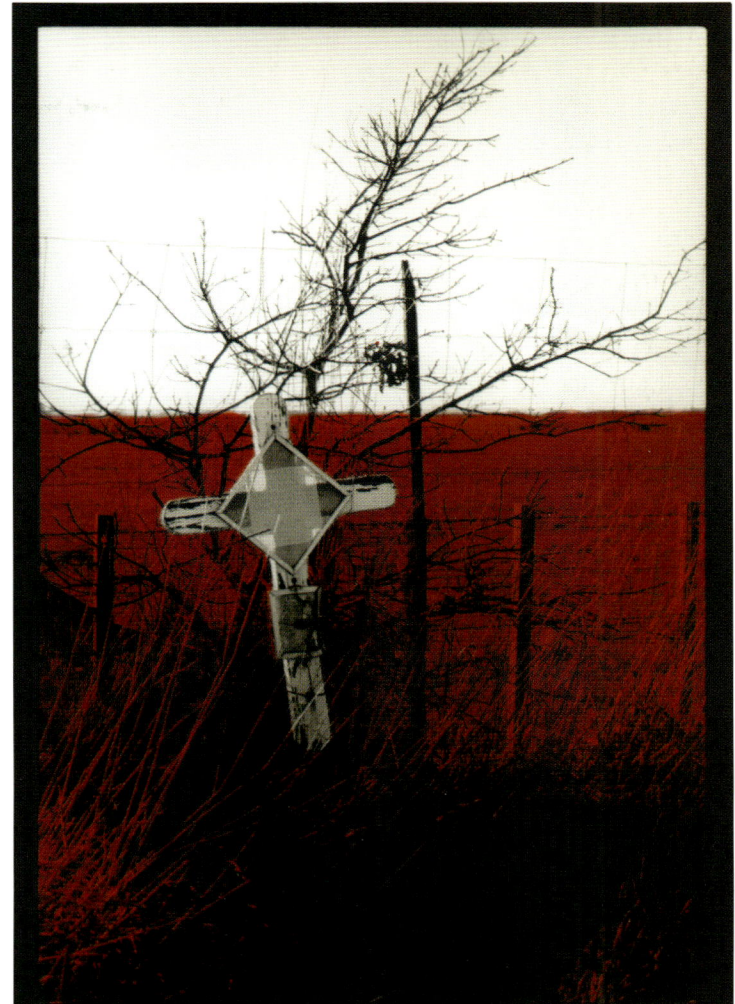

years, an uncle's fence-jumping and so on. In contrast to the anonymity of the non-place, some rural inhabitants are born, live and die in communities of robust personhood and widely shared personal histories. A rural person's identity may be as much social (e.g. linked to family) as it is individual. I spent many of my own formative years in a small community, leaving at age 18 for the bright lights of Wellington, Auckland, London and beyond. After more than a decade away I returned briefly and was reincorporated into the community as the eldest son of my well-known parents (my father is a life member of the rugby club, my mother an icon in the local Lotto shop). At this time my first child, Corinna, was born. It was late one Saturday night and my parents, together with most of my extended family, were holidaying in Taupo. I phoned my parents with news of their first grandchild and they duly informed our relatives in Taupo, but did not contact anyone else — and neither did I. Yet the following Monday morning I was congratulated by a local bank teller whom I did not personally know and who, without prompting, accurately recounted the day and time my daughter was born, her birth weight and the list of names we were considering. In a similar vein a few long-time residents in Martinborough have formed an informal yet highly effective group to assist community members who have been recently widowed or who are struggling with the trials of old age. Rural or small communities can be places where knowledge and experiences are widely shared, where social ties are intimate and enduring. Thus, rural spaces can carry great meaning — areas which to urban eyes appear to be little more than undifferentiated pasture (i.e. archetypal non-places that are hastily passed in a journey between A and B) may be strongly identified with friends and families of the past, present and future. In many rural communities everyone not only knows your name, but also your place.

This type of social intimacy is even more pronounced in the many small-scale, descent-based societies that anthropologists typically study. For instance, the Trobriand Islanders of Melanesia trace their clan or *dala* links through the female line. The clans are land-owning corporations which determine an individual's access to resources and choice of spouse, as they must marry outside of their birth clan. As the clans are territorial they also dictate where an individual will live, with young children living in the villages of their father's clan. However, from adolescence — and in order to provide the next crop of senior male members — all boys live in the territory of their *dala* or birth clan (i.e. their mother's people). In contrast, girls remain with their father's household until marriage, from which time they must join their husband's people. Ideally, as a man's sons are leaving, his sister's sons are joining him. The clans are also ranked as either chiefly or common, so birth determines an individual's status, prestige and power. Throughout their entire lives the rank, roles, responsibilities and social acts of individual Trobrianders are largely prescribed by specific norms of descent, marriage, gender and age.

Although many of us would baulk at the social constraints

experienced daily by individual Trobrianders, we also resist the obscurity of the non-place that accompanies our high-speed pursuit of exalted individualism. Such resistance exists whenever an All Black plays for passion and not money. It exists in warming to the smile of your child, in sharing a meal with a loved one, in standing still. It exists in planting a tree and watching it grow to maturity. It even exists in world-weary urbanites who sit and chat with rural homestay operators, or in friendships that transcend the commercial realities of the workplace. The white roadside crosses also attempt to resist the numbing anonymity of the non-place and non-personhood. Without these crosses our loved ones would die as nameless travellers, unknowable strangers. With only broken fences — which are promptly repaired — to mark a mortal passing, the crosses remind us of complete lives lived and lost. A simple white cross pays homage to the intimacy of Steve and Lorraine, who are eulogised by friends and family as real and much loved people. They ask that other travellers pause and ponder the true value of their humanity, the humanity of their loved ones … of all loved ones. The crosses mark the tension between the intimacy of home and the sterility of the non-place. Yet for those who daily speed by in their cars, the crosses are little more than a blur of white. To them Steve and Lorraine are irrelevant. Simply non-people who once passed through — and away — in a non-place.

Signposts for you to follow … or ignore

Augé M (1995) *Non-places: introduction to an anthropology of supermodernity*, London, Verso

Cohen AP (ed, 1985) *The Symbolic Construction of Community*, London, Tavistock Publications

Faith N (1990) *The World the Railways Made*, London, Pimlico

Gellner E (1983) *Nations and Nationalism*, Oxford, Blackwell

Giddens A (1991) *Modernity and Self-identity*, Cambridge, Polity

King M (1985) *Being Pakeha: an encounter with Maori renaissance*, Auckland, Hodder & Stoughton

Ings W & A Fox (2001) 'Roadside crosses: a memorial and a message' *New Zealand Geographic*, 54: 58-67

Malinowski B (1961) *Argonauts of the Western Pacific: an account of native enterprise and adventure in the archipelagoes of Melanesian New Guinea*, London, Dutton

Somerset H (1938) *Littledene: a New Zealand rural community*, Wellington, New Zealand Council for Educational Research

— (1974) *Littledene: patterns of change*, Wellington, New Zealand Council for Educational Research

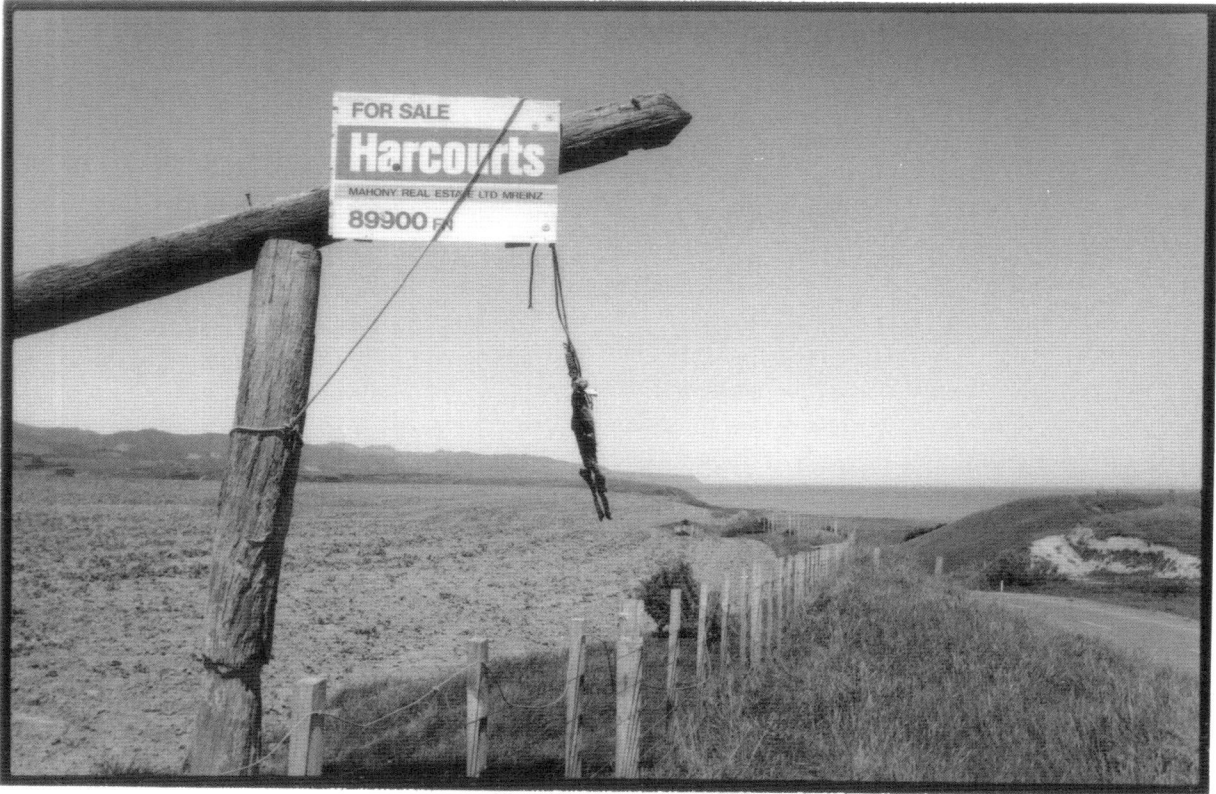

VIII
THE SUPERMARKET, THE NET, AND THE STARLINGS
PLACE, SPACE, SYMBOLS & ACTION

I HAD JUST SETTLED down for a cuppa after a morning's hard graft when the Martinborough winemaker I was with stood bolt upright. "I'll get the gun!" he cried as he ran off towards the winery. On his return he strode to the nearest row of vines, lifted the .22 and blasted off several rounds. Back at the smoko table he grumbled that the third starling had escaped. I had watched in awe — I hadn't seen any birds, I couldn't see where the dead birds lay and if one had managed to flee it was news to me. I knew that starlings and other birds send scouts into a vineyard to test whether it's safe for an entire flock to follow. It was vital not to let the first birds return with the news of rapidly ripening grapes. But no matter how hard I looked, I was blind to the birds. I remained a vineyard klutz, out of place and virtually able to step on starlings before they flew mockingly away.

Places are the cultural settings in which our social lives happen and they exist on continuums from the physical to the rhetorical; the known to the imagined; the backyard to the universe. Many of us are unaware of how much we create place through our beliefs and actions, and correspondingly how place creates us through its influence on our behaviour. In anthropology there is an increasing awareness that the study of place can help us to understand culture and society. During my research on the vineyard, the sophistication and intricacies of the winemaker's knowledge of his bacchanalian domain amazed me. To say that he knew his vineyard like the back of his hand was an understatement. No matter where we were in the vineyard he could always identify the soil type, the microclimate, the clones planted. Once the grapes had been pressed and their juice barrelled he could take the smallest sip and detect where the grapes had been picked. That he had such an intimate knowledge of his vineyard while I remained a myopic oaf bears testament to the importance of place in our everyday lives.

The more experience we have of a certain place, the more effectively we respond to its complexities and subtleties. On the vineyard I was out-of-place; the winemaker was in-place. He had built it from scratch, driving hundreds of posts into stony ground, planting thousands of vines and nurturing them season after season. Yet even after 20 years he still laments his lack of experience, especially with the seasonal vagaries that critically impact on his craft. As the vines mature and send roots ever deeper in search of nutrients, the dynamics of viticulture and winemaking constantly change. Thus, the winemaker's knowledge of his vineyard is forever partial; he is always learning something new.

Since infancy we have been learning, often unconsciously, how to read, respond to, and behave in the different places of New Zealand. The shared understandings that come from this education are the core of our collective existence. We'd probably all agree on what is inside or outside, up or down, private or public. We further share a culture by being able to distinguish between a massage parlour and a post shop — irrespective of whether we personally use such places. Anyone who confuses the two and tries to mail a letter in a brothel or get extras at the post shop will either be rebuked or hailed as a ground-breaker. Similarly, when we enter a church, a museum or an art gallery — all sacred places of one form or another — most of us tend to talk quietly and act in a thoughtful, reverential manner, whatever our personal belief systems or interests.

Sharing a culture goes far beyond such elementary understandings, as we learn to read place like a complex text full of signs, metaphors and messages. As we enter a restaurant, a park or a rugby stadium we — mostly unconsciously — read the spatial symbols and work out the social context. Then we act and interact in keeping with the roles which apply to our age, gender,

class, etc. For example, a TAB is a space — usually inhabited by taciturn men intently studying thumb-worn racebooks — which up till the late 1980s was clearly marked off from purer pursuits by being hidden behind opaque windows. Nowadays TABs are more open, but tend to be in stand-alone premises, distinct from the more widely-accepted commercial ventures such as clothing stores or insurance firms. This contrasts dramatically with Lotto outlets, which are integral to bookshops, supermarkets and malls, visited by all manner of men, women and children. Hence, Lotto is generally thought of as harmless fun, on a par with the normal economic pursuits of retail shopping or sharemarket dabbling. In essence, the isolation of the TAB pigeonholes gambling on sports, horse and dog racing as a vice — or at best an irrational form of recreation. The only other place a TAB is welcome is in public bars — historically sites for men to pursue that unholy trinity of vice: gambling, alcohol and illicit sex. In contrast, the lingerie department is still mainly the preserve of females, the kindergarten sandpit is a child's space and New Zealand is the home territory of passport-packing Kiwis.

Spaces are the physical settings in which different social contexts occur — in other words, the social and cultural use of space creates *place*. A kitchen is a space designed as a place where food is prepared. Depending on the social use of the kitchen table it can change from a place where meals are shared to one where kids do homework or where the postman always knocks twice. Similarly, by day Vivian Street in Wellington and K Road in Auckland are sites for retail therapy and skateboarding, but by night they become places of prostitution, drug dealing and skateboarding.

Cultural perspectives of place change over time. As late as the 18th century many Europeans thought mountains were infested with evil dragons. The pious of the West did not shun mountains altogether, as many nobles and priests proved their faith or heavenly favour by going to slay — or at least survive an encounter with — a dragon. By the end of the 19th century most European cultures had given away such beliefs. Mountains came to be seen as sites of adventure, leisure and even — in the case of ascents of specially testing peaks — proof of enlightened man's domination of nature. They were also viewed as places of political ascendancy, hence the debate over whether Ed Hillary or Tenzing Norgay was the first to scale Mt Everest in 1953. With Hillary being a New Zealand citizen, Tenzing a Nepalese and the whole jaunt funded and led by British concerns, controversy still simmers over which nation could claim this particular slice of elevated glory. When counterclaims — such as that Englishmen George Mallory and Andrew Irvine were actually the first to reach the summit in 1924 — are added to the mix it seems that the dispute over the individual and political subjugation of Mt Everest will fester for some time yet.

When differences in the social use of place confront us we can become highly aware of our own habits or norms. As my mentor James Urry states: "You don't know how wet you are until you get out of the pool." Many Pakeha (and a few urbanised Maori) have strong out-of-place feelings when entering a Maori marae for the first few times. By virtue of living in New Zealand some of us are aware that different areas on a marae are *noa* (profane) or *tapu* (sacred) and that others are more or less male or female areas. Aside from knowing that it is offensive to sit on any table or bench where food will be prepared or eaten — and that shoes must removed before entering the meeting house (wharenui) — few Pakeha know much about behaviours which are appropriate on different marae and how this may vary on specific occasions. In being out-of-place on a marae, people may become acutely and nervously aware of their bodies — of where they put their hands, where they focus their eyes, how they walk and perform other actions.

Once I arrived at a marae unannounced, for an interview. It was mid-morning and there was no sign of activity. I had an idea of protocols for formal occasions but knew nothing of everyday life on a marae. I remember breaking out in a sweat as I walked up the path towards the wharenui. I had no idea of whether I was allowed to approach from the front unannounced or whether I should step on to the porch and knock on the closed door. Fortunately someone in the kitchen spotted my Mr Bean routine as I hopped on and off pathways, up and down porches, and came to my rescue with an offer of a cup of tea. Until that moment I was a real Pakeha out-of-his-car.

In formal ceremonies an individual from the host marae may be appointed to guide guests through the ritual welcome. This — combined with the nascent knowledge of Maori culture that many Pakeha have — can relieve the anxiety that arises from such unfamiliarity. Yet whenever we are out-of-place the nervousness or culture shock we may experience shows just how much we genuinely inhabit space. Places are saturated with various cultural ideas and social actions; with different habits and thus different inhabitants.

The Kwaio of the Solomon Islands, who build their villages on the sides of steep mountains along a vertical axis, have spatial domains that dominate their lives. The highest point of the village is the most sacred realm and is where shrines are built for the ritual sacrifice of pigs to ancestors or *adalo*. Only adult men can enter this realm, as women's bodies are thought to be polluting — menstrual and childbirth fluids are seen as extremely contaminating. Failure to follow the correct ritual or observe the rigid pollution taboos surrounding women is believed to anger the *adalo* and cause them to bring sickness or death on their descendants. The middle or domestic section of the village is the realm of gardening, eating and sleeping. Menstruating women or those about to give birth must separate themselves from it. They are confined to the purpose-built huts placed at the lowest point of the settlements which are the exclusive preserve of adult women.

Kwaio settlements are organised according to the following social, religious and spatial boundaries:

Female : Male
Polluted : Sacred
Down : Up

Much of Kwaio life is occupied in ensuring that the sacred, domestic and polluted realms are demarcated at all times. The men's house, where adult men sleep and eat, is in the upper part of the village and close to the adalo shrines — also off-limits to women. Even in the middle of the village the uphill side of each domestic hut is forbidden to women. Women must never be physically above men nor stand over cooking pots when preparing food, lest they pollute men with their bodily essences. Men who have sex with women must undergo purification rituals to cleanse themselves before they return to the men's house and clan shrines. Women who move down to the menstrual area must leave their smoking pipes and bags in the domestic realm to avoid cross-contamination on their return.

Although the Kwaio's experience of place appears dominated by social-religious forces, we often underestimate the complexity, nuance and influence that place asserts in our everyday lives. A trip to the supermarket reveals much more than the economics and physical logistics of buying the week's groceries. Supermarkets are laden with sophisticated spatial symbols, values and moralities, many of which we respond to in unconscious and habitual ways. When entering a supermarket we first meet the fresh fruit and vegetables. This placement makes little practical sense, as many of these products easily damage under the weight of other groceries. Together with the clever use of mirrors, lighting and misted water, it taps into the primal symbolism of hunter-gatherer societies where individuals are believed to roam widely and freely in their search for nutritious fruits, vegetables and nuts. It also engages the romantic idea that many in the middle classes share about the abundant goodness of nature — of trees groaning with ripe exotic fruits on faraway tropical islands.

The exaltation of nature at the beginning of a shopping expedition is matched by an equal celebration of culture at the other end of the supermarket. The evolution of culture can be seen as a sophisticated attempt to capture and cook nature — the domestication of plants and animals to ensure a ready supply of food. The ability to release nutrients and enhance flavours of food through the intentional use of fire is also at the heart of culture. To make and break bread, to hunt and roast giraffe, to raise and broil chickens — to catch or nurture food, then cook and eat it together — is a central part of social life. The weary shopper, tired from the work of hunting and gathering groceries and looking forward to carting their hard-bought spoils home, discovers the bakery near the end of their supermarket trip. The sweet, homely smell of baking bread is tantalisingly redolent of home and hearth — a celebration of culture's most beneficial dominion over nature.

Before we're overcome with collective sentiment, we should recall that the supermarket layout is also designed to express social and class differences. Cheaper products — from generic baked beans to budget toothbrushes — tend to be shelved low and the more expensive products high, giving messages about

A trip to the supermarket reveals much more than the economics and physical logistics of buying the week's groceries.

social status. Similarly, dearer cuts of meat are shown under glass like precious jewels, to be individually scrutinised and chosen by the discerning shopper. Cheaper cuts of meat are lumped together in cellophane wrap and stacked in open-top freezers for the hoi polloi.

The ethos of the middle classes, that individual hard work should be rewarded and that the mind-numbing banality of the daily grind should be alleviated with frequent play, is also echoed in supermarket layout. Specials on biscuits, chocolates and tasty titbits are usually found at the end of aisles — rewards for the hard work of shopping for staple foods and products. Likewise, when the total work of shopping is done you are further enticed to treat yourself to discretionary pleasure items — mags, fags and sweets — at the checkout counters. This analysis doesn't even begin to consider the gendered sections of tampons and cosmetics, batteries and lightbulbs; or the symbolism of toilet paper embossed with images of playful dolphins.

Although the supermarket may contain a range of areas — which cater to different notions of age, gender, class and social circumstances — other places are less equivocal in the messages they convey. As a mature university student raising a young family my bank balance has at times fallen well short of the bourgeois ideal. As a result I have experienced the varied joys and trials of dental care in the private and public sectors. One of the first things that struck me as I passed from uptown to downtown dental surgeries was the spatial class dimensions of their waiting rooms. Dental surgeries for the poor are usually found down forlorn alleys — bespeckled with graffiti and used as carparks for the businesses that tower above, eclipsing the midday sun. Their waiting rooms offer little more in the way of comfort — walls are either a drab off-green or insipid brown. The few indoor plants, dying in their plastic pots, look like leftovers from a flat-moving. Any furniture is well past its best-by date — stuffing falls out of cushions and stains overlay one another to mask the original weave. Nothing is co-ordinated. Wood, cane and metal-ribbed chairs plucked from disparate decades jostle for bums, bags and sniffling children. The magazines are old and well-thumbed, ranging from a *Women's Weekly* featuring a fresh-faced 19-year-old Rachel Hunter (circa 1989) to a local council policy document on services for the financially challenged (also out of date). Faded, corner-torn posters askew on the walls promote the best practice in gum maintenance, sexual disease prevention, domestic abuse awareness and recycling — constant reminders that poverty need not lower moral standards.

Then there is the other squeeze of the mint-fresh toothpaste. After receiving a gilt-edged reminder card and a mock-cheerful phonecall that your six-monthly checkup is due you glide up to the private dental surgery in an old Victorian villa with clipped privet hedges and intricate brick pathways or in a central city high-rise that is all plush carpet, tinted windows and high-speed elevators. The private dental surgery immerses you in a world of order, cleanliness and precision. Large yucca plants in glazed ceramic pots are tastefully placed in the corners of the waiting room. Original prints by well-known artists adorn the walls, contrasting pleasingly with the pastel wallpaper. Slinky armchairs — colour and style co-ordinated — await to comfort the anxious patient, while the rimu coffee table features a tidy pile of the latest *Time, Business Review* and daily paper. A discreet pamphlet display on one wall offers the latest in health and dental insurance, while Vivaldi's *Four Seasons* wafts gently out of the surgery.

The evolution of culture can be seen as an ever more sophisticated attempt to capture and cook nature

Similar contrasts exist between public and private schools. Even from their gates the division is clear. Private schools have stout brick walls and freshly mown, lush green fields — public schools have six-strand wire fences that surround a muddy playing-field. Then there are private and public hospitals. The former feature single rooms complete with garden outlooks and TVs. The latter are ghastly mazes of long, draughty corridors, crowded mixed-sex wards and tatty common rooms stuffed full of relatives, wheelchairs, scattered building blocks and a single TV with poor reception. This comparison of spatial-symbolic dynamics highlights stark differences in class, wealth and resources. Such symbolism, however, only conveys a *sense* of advantage — proof ultimately lies in the practices of place. My worst dental encounter (half a pulled tooth inadvertently left in my gum) was endured at the hands of a highly expensive dentist. In a similar vein the homes of New Zealand's middle classes often convey a sense of prosperity, refined taste or cultured intellect. That is, at least, in the public areas of the home — the lounge, kitchen and common bathrooms. Backstage, in the *en suite* bathroom cupboard, at the bottom of the bedroom wardrobe or even under the master bed, it may be different story altogether as the *New Zealand Historical Atlas* is succeeded by the battery-powered purple love-rocket.

Many spaces contain contradictory values and practices, as we see in the history of European rural places and people. The countryside has long been seen as a bucolic, tranquil and picturesque site of idyllic agrarian life, but it has also been denigrated as a rustic, uncouth and backward home for inbred hicks. Generally, if urban places are seen as modern and dynamic, then rural places are likely to be cast in a lesser light, and vice versa. You may, however, simultaneously hold opposing views, believing that although the city is a site of dynamic creativity, it pollutes nature and corrupts social relations. Thus you may seek periodic rural retreat to restore balance and harmony to your life.

In the wine village of Martinborough in the Wairarapa these varied responses to rurality can be seen in the way urbanites engage with the town. Many visitors to Martinborough have moved permanently there to retire; others come to work in wine or olives or to raise young families away from the city's hurly-burly. Some show their commitment to the community by joining local clubs or school-related groups. Other urbanites — known wryly as 'two-day locals' — have weekend baches, yet are gradually supplanting full-timers. In 1991 Martinborough had 1506 residents — today that has declined to 1356, although the total number of houses is about the same. Two-day locals also celebrate the rurality of Martinborough, but not so much. They may make friends with locals, but often only with those who enhance their weekends (e.g. winemakers, the golf club secretary). In other circumstances many regard the locals as country bumpkins and bemoan their lack of sophistication.

A third set of urbanites simply travel to Martinborough at weekends, in private cars or on bus tours. If they stay over they rent a homestay or motel. Travelling with friends or family, the countryside is little more than a nice backdrop to their rural incursion and they avoid in-depth contact with residents. Some may eventually move to Martinborough for good or on a weekend-bach basis, and if they still wish to keep up the social barriers they can choose the relative sanctuary of a gated subdivision. Notions of Hicksville are often as much imagined as they are real. People encountering Martinborough locals are often surprised at the richness and range of their life experiences. The farmer leaning over the fence is likely to have travelled on foot through Africa, served in the diplomatic corps or trained as an airforce pilot.

Yet we live in a world where imagined environments are

routinely made 'real' through literature, TV, the internet and film. More than ever we can — through such media — share our experiences of place with others who may be physically absent. Travellers from afar can visit Martinborough in person using the communication pathways of planes, trains and automobiles. Or they can use other information highways and experience the town through the internet on www.martinborough.co.nz or in a *Lonely Planet* guidebook. In many respects Martinborough has never been a mere physically-bounded place or entity. Established in the 1880s by John Martin, the town was laid out in the form of the Union Jack in homage to Martin's birthplace. He named streets after places he visited on his grand tour of Europe and the US — so today you experience echoes of New York and Cologne strolling through Martinborough. This fuzziness of place — in which signposts to absent places are part and parcel of the township — resonates in the names of its contemporary homestays, e.g. *The Venice Affair* or *Dublin House*.

Some social pundits proclaim that technologies such as TV, the internet and global travel challenge the role and salience of local place. They argue that individuals increasingly draw on a vast body of references to construct their worlds, from the physical intimacy of your own backyard to the conceptual knowledge of other places gleaned from TV docos. Some post-modernists even believe that the internet — which is here, there, everywhere and nowhere at the same time — democratises place by enabling a gamut of perspectives to be simultaneously ex-pressed. Moreover, multiple referencing shows how gender, class, age, ethnicity, sexuality, disability etc can produce contrasting ideas, values and practices of place. Many now believe that places are better thought of as texts we personally interpret and inscribe (better, that is, for the erstwhile academics who find such convol-utions fertile grounds for analysis, re-analysis, re-re-analysis …).

But wait up. As our referential worlds have expanded, the *local* has paradoxically become more important. As our eyes open to worlds of difference, we not only become more aware of how others are distinct, but we are also encouraged to identify (and commodify) our own uniqueness. Winemakers promote their pinot noir as a unique, seasonal expression of their vineyard's specific *terroir* — an expression that cannot be exactly duplicated in any other place or time. Hence the label on the bottle carries details of vintage and vineyard location. We may be able to inscribe or interpret place as a text, but this is different from the grounded reality of place actually being a text. As any gardener knows, familiarity with a picture of a plant is not the same thing as trying to grow a tree in your backyard. Similarly, a tree falling in the forest may or may not make a sound. Yet if you happen to be standing under a tree when it falls then your ruminations are likely to be abruptly ended — and this is irrespective of whether your internet chatgroup has finished debating the metaphysical dilemmas posed by falling trees.

Beliefs that the internet and other communication pathways can democratise space also make a mockery of individuals in the so-called Third World. Most of the world's poor do not have access to the net. Only 600 million — or less than 15% of us —

have access, with the bulk of the world's users found in the USA, Canada, Europe and Asia/Pacific (93%). Africa accounts for only 0.8% or 4.2 million users. The 2001 New Zealand census revealed that 37% of households had internet access, although this was mediated by wealth — 7 out of every 10 households enjoying incomes of more than $100,000 had internet, compared with only 1 in 9 households with incomes of $10,001 to $15,000.

Certainly the most popular websites draw massive audiences. CyberErotica's site averages over 250,000 hits a day, amassing a staggering 2 billion hits since it opened in 1996. Yet this pales in comparison with the facts of life for half of the world's population. The World Bank Group — a conservative apologist for global capitalism — estimates that 2.5 billion individuals struggle to survive on less than NZ$5 a day, with 1.3 billion living on less than NZ$2.50. More than 2.9 billion lack adequate sanitation and 1.2 billion live without safe water. No matter how the internet may democratise space, place, sex, identity or anything else, the simple fact is that for the world's poor there is a brutal reality to their localised experience of place, cruelly apparent whenever their wells run dry, crops fail, stomachs ache with hunger or bodies are racked by disease. Martinborough winemakers have a similar — but obviously much more pleasant — material experience of place whenever they plant and nurture seedlings to maturity. And both rich and poor know their place in the world in ways that images or words can never convey, no matter how seductive, sharp and savvy the new *iPhoto* technology.

Keep your feet firmly referenced to the ground:

Ben-Ari E & Y Bilu (eds, 1997) *Grasping Land: space and place in contemporary Israeli discourse and experience*, Albany, State University of New York Press

Ching B & G Creed (eds, 1997) *Knowing your Place: rural identity and cultural hierarchy*, New York, Routledge

Cooper M (2002) *Wine Atlas of New Zealand*, Auckland, Hodder Moa Beckett

Gupta A & J Ferguson (eds, 1997) *Culture, Power, Place: explorations in critical anthropology*, Durham, NC, Duke University Press

Hirsch E & M O'Hanlon (eds, 1995) *The Anthropology of Landscape: perspectives on place and space*, Oxford, Clarendon Press

Keesing R (1982) *Kwaio Religion: the living and the dead in a Solomon Island society*, New York, Columbia University Press

Schama S (1995) *Landscape and Memory*, New York, Knopf

Urry J (1995) *Consuming Places*, New York, Routledge

Williams R (1973) *The Country and the City*, London, Chatto & Windus

IX

MARTINBOROUGH'S PINOT PILGRIMS:
RURAL ESCAPISM AND MONASTERIES OF CONSUMPTION

WINE, TOURISM, CLASS & THE IDEAL SELF

I WAS WORKING AT THE Martinborough Information Centre as part of my research into wine tourism when a late-model Toyota Camry pulled up outside. A short time later a middle-aged man dressed in Rodd & Gunn bustled through the front entrance and breathlessly asked if I knew the way to Ata Rangi and Martinborough vineyards. Before I could reply he launched into an euphoric monologue of how he had travelled up from Christchurch specifically to visit the vineyards. With visible pride he recalled that on his journey north, through a friend's personal contact, he had met with Kevin Judd, the widely respected winemaker at Cloudy Bay in Marlborough. Although he didn't have any local links, meeting the winemakers at Ata Rangi and Martinborough vineyards would be the highlight of his wine career. Did I know the winemakers and were they approachable? I assured him that he would be well received and sent him off with a map of Martinborough's vineyards to navigate from shrine to shrine.

Since the late 1980s Martinborough has become a mecca for pinot noir enthusiasts and a popular retreat for jaded urbanites seeking relief from the bustle of city living. From overnighters to two-day locals (lifestylers with weekend properties and shiny four-wheel drives), thousands flock to the small rural township in search of peace and tranquillity. Most travel the hour and a bit from Wellington to visit Martinborough in the South Wairarapa region, which is currently marketed as the 'Capital Country Escape.' Many visit Martinborough to enjoy the wines, the countryside and the weather (this being a given as Wellingtonians rarely venture out if it is raining on the other side of the Rimutakas). At the information centre, requests for accommodation are often for colonial cottages with open fires and baths big enough for two. Around 90% of visitors to Martinborough who have dependent children are likely to leave them behind, and many hosts in the area are reluctant to accommodate children, or ban them altogether.

At first glance none of this appears startling. Anyone raising a family knows the need for quality time away from their anklebiters. Rural holidays have a long history that directly links centuries-old villas in Tuscany with baches in the Coromandel, and wine tourism throughout the Western world is increasingly popular among the affluent. Wine tourism in New Zealand centres around the boutique vineyard. Of the 421 wineries registered with the New Zealand Wine Institute in 2003, 394 or 93% produced less than 200,000 litres annually. Large wineries such as Montana regularly yield more than 2 million litres per year. To put this into an even more meaningful global perspective — New Zealand wineries supply 0.2% of the world's wine. In 2000 our vineyards produced approximately 60 million litres — compared with Australia's more than 800 million and the top-hooch French with more than 6200 million. The world's largest winemaker, Gallo in California, produces more than New Zealand and Australia combined — more than 1300 million litres annually.

> *Others earnestly seek friendships with boutique winemakers — delighting in their tales of the hard toil and extraordinary vision required to produce nature's heady nectar.*

Yet the modesty of our wineries is a major part of their appeal. Many people shun large, mass-produced and impersonally marketed vino in the hope of finding little-known vineyards making fine, handcrafted wines. Others earnestly seek friendships with boutique winemakers — delighting in their tales of the hard toil and extraordinary vision required to produce nature's heady nectar. A personalised visit to a boutique winery can intensify your sense of individuality, as you take away unique memories and stories (not to mention wines) to impress friends and thereby increase your social status on your return home.

Many winemakers grasp the value of this personal touch and about 83% provide cellar-door sales, despite these accounting for only 20% of total turnover. Potential spinoffs are realised whenever an individual tries to recapture the magic of their visit by buying the same brand of wine at their supermarket, restaurant or in response to the vineyard's mail-outs. More spinoffs come whenever a vineyard visitor provides a word-of-mouth plug to a friend, chef or corporate bigwig.

Anthropologists take nothing for granted and Martinborough's increasing popularity invites investigation. With regard to tourism in Martinborough, two issues leap out. Firstly, why don't people simply buy Martinborough wines at urban liquor outlets and drink them at home? Secondly, why do so many visitors not bring their dependent children to Martinborough?

The latter question is especially relevant as many Kiwi urbanites believe that rural places represent some type of Arcadia — sites of natural beauty, timelessness and simplicity. Places of honest toil and wholesome products, where families and friends work, play and live together in relative harmony. In contrast, cities are often thought of as polluted soulless environments populated by unknowable strangers. The desire for a Golden Past of rural community and neighbourliness may partly explain requests to stay in the township's colonial cottages. But it doesn't explain why tourists contradict the family-focused ideals of agrarian life by excluding their own rugrats. Nor does it explain the link between wine, cottages, open fires, bathtubs and these absent children. Interestingly, analysis of this *mélange* didn't occur to me until I too was absent from Martinborough and in a very different social setting — listening to an American sociologist discussing the global phenomenon of McDonald's. Most of his analysis of the mass-produced food, generic service and universal architecture had little to do with Martinborough's tourism and wine industries, but it nevertheless inspired this analysis.

Martinborough tourists are for the most part resolutely middle-class. My survey of them has shown that:

- About 55% of the males had annual incomes of more than NZ$50,000, with 13% enjoying more than NZ$95,000. What's more, 24% of the females had incomes of more than NZ$40,000 and 3.4% more than NZ$95,000. This compares with the average wage in New Zealand, which currently hovers around NZ$35,000 — though 30% get less than NZ$10,000 per annum.
- Nearly 60% had university degrees, 65% described themselves as professionals and more than 75% described themselves as New Zealand European or Pakeha.
- The main reason for their visit was to see the vineyards and taste wine. Doh!
- 43% came with friends and 37% with family. My survey of

homestays in the area also showed that around 60% of bookings were for couples.

A more comprehensive survey of wine tourism in New Zealand has produced similar results — 46% enjoyed annual incomes of more than NZ$50,000 (21% with more than NZ$80,000); 62% described themselves as professionals and 48% had a university degree.

> *Martinborough's tourists are latter-day Romantics … who seek their sacred or authentic selves in an enchanted rural setting.*

While these statistics may classify our wine tourists according to a variety of social and economic measures, they do not reveal the cultural values, beliefs or sentiments that may be central to their bacchanalian rambles. My view is that they are latter-day Romantics whose holidays *really are* holy days, where they seek an encounter with their sacred or authentic selves in an enchanted rural setting. The 18th century Romantic movement coincided with and was at odds with the industrial revolution that was sweeping Europe. The Romantics, whose members were drawn from the emerging middle classes and above, greatly favoured rural life, countryside rambles and poetic musings on the bounteous joys of nature. They saw city existence as profane and rural life as sacred. The Romantics believed the self to be divine and that personal experience, especially gratifying feelings, was fundamental to the authentic expression of self. They also sought immediate — as opposed to heavenly — salvation and would dash off into the countryside or on grand tours of Greek sites of antiquity to find their true inner selves. All this would be recorded in rapturous sonnets dedicated to self-love and the gods or goddesses of nature. Our romance with things pastoral in New Zealand clearly extends beyond watching lambs gambol around spring pastures, to include winemaking in rural spaces. According to Jancis Robinson's *Oxford Companion to Wine*, the term 'lifestyle winery' was actually coined in New Zealand to refer to a small winery established more for its bucolic appeal than as a commercial enterprise, typically run by an educated young to middle-aged couple.

Current desire for the rural in New Zealand can range from contemplating the aesthetics of dairy cows to actual social engagement with country life. On a bus tour to Martinborough a group entered a local vineyard and noticed a dead lamb in a nearby paddock. Many were so disturbed that they would not sample the vineyard's products, fearing that the beast might have somehow contaminated the wine. When I asked one of them why they found this sight so revolting, especially considering that on any farm there will regularly be dead animals, she replied: "That's not the point — it's simply bad marketing." Other urbanites will look beyond such romantic blind spots, and in Martinborough a couple of hundred have taken up residence in recent years. They include weekenders, retirees, lifestyle farmers, boutique vignerons and olive planters.

Some show their commitment to rural life by joining local groups such as Lions or Rotary. Yet the fastest growing club in town is the Wine & Food Society, which boasts a membership of more than one hundred: about 10% of the town. This club's main aim is to scoff food and wine in the company of like-palated individuals. In contrast with older service clubs, their focus is on individual pleasure rather than societal or business concerns. Talk of farm mortgages, seasonal labour supply, falling school rolls and the provision of rural social services in an increasingly centralised New Zealand rarely disrupts the good-life practices of the Wine & Food Society.

As discussed above, many of Martinborough's recent visitors come from the professional ranks and tend to reproduce the Romantic sense of the divine self. While the middle classes draw on collective concepts of gender, class, age, ethnicity and sexual preference for their identities, their educational, work and daily lives nevertheless promote the autonomous individual. Many actively plot their futures, using personal skills and knowledge to fulfil their desires. Hence the current popularity of upmarket gyms, self-help books and career development programmes, all of which endorse self-determination, growth and the pursuit of individual happiness. To many, the popular decrees to *Be somebody* or *Just do it* are not just catchy advertising jingles, they are moral mantras that guide the quest for personal fulfilment.

While many gain a great deal of satisfaction from their occupational and social lives, the Kiwi middle classes also regularly experience denial of the true self. Many feel they are little more than interchangeable cogs in the machinery of commerce, with their personal creativity and decision-making capabilities seriously compromised. Domestic chores — buying groceries, clothing children and cleaning the toilet, let alone life-partners who take a more jaundiced view of your exalted self-worth — can also negate spontaneous celebrations of individuality. When people complain of being trapped at work, at home, by marriage or mortgage, they highlight the extent to which their social and economic circumstances curb the expression of their real selves. Like the 18th century Romantics, many Kiwis clearly believe the self is sacred and that any denial of the self is sacrilegious.

The ethics of today's consumerism — or retail therapy as it is more popularly known — also parallel some key tenets of 18th century Romanticism. Both share the ideals of unlimited good and consider that individuals are ethically obliged to better themselves by seeking out and satisfying new wants. The conspicuous — and credit-card-fuelled — consumption of clothing, food, cars and leisure events lets individuals express their perfect selves in arenas that transcend the limits of work, home and bank balances. The way new cars are promoted exults this ethos. Every year advertisers proclaim that new cars offer a range of benefits: more comfort, better performance, greater safety, increased social status and even enhanced sex appeal for the buyer. Although most cars in New Zealand end up on urban roads, ads depict them in rural or wilderness settings. This links with the Romantic belief in the authenticity of nature — the new car embodies the natural expression of the individual. Similarly, many younger Kiwis seek to express their authentic selves in adrenalin-pumping activities like bungy jumping and rock climbing. While these activities take place in rural or natural settings, there is no technical reason they could not be done in urban environs. Rurality or nature legitimates these apparently death-defying activities as authentic tests of the spirit — never mind that most are probably less dangerous than driving on a busy urban highway.

Furthermore, most people consume at an aesthetic level. Social significance is widely attached to appearances, enabling individuals to respond quickly to changes in fashions and fads — swapping the company-leased Audi for a soft-top Porsche in time for fun summer motoring. Keeping up with current trends and gratifying new consumer wants — whether the latest in DVD players or adult scooters — is one way the middle classes evince their personal knowledge of, and proficiency in, contemporary life. It is much more difficult to align the perfect self with changes in other areas. If being single, black and a nuclear physicist suddenly became hip, it would be almost impossible for most of us to quickly change careers, alter our genes and divorce our spouses to take advantage of this particular trend. Indeed, as most materialism is aesthetic, the ideals it expresses are often illusory. Middle-aged men who drive sports cars, wear Versace and seek to impress with platinum Amex cards, may or may not be as virile as their public acts of consumption suggest. Likewise they may not own the car and flashing a platinum does not necessarily denote the ability to pay the monthly bill. However, as one wit noted, individuals are increasingly encouraged to be "serfs at work and kings in the supermarket." These days we work so we can play at being ourselves. After the responsibilities of work and home have been discharged, denied or fobbed off, thousands express their true selves by shopping till they drop or by shaking their booty in the flattering lights of the local nightclub.

The making and drinking of wine eloquently expresses the quest for variety that underpins the middle class's consumerism and related romantic quests to find their true selves. Wine is innately a highly variable product. Not only does it vary from region to region, year to year, clone to clone, winemaker to winemaker — it also evolves in the bottle. Varieties like pinot noir may only reach their peak after five or more years. Not surprisingly then, many of us aspire to own or at least know about such fine wine as a sign of our capacity to keep up with trends and fashions in the world of the oenophile. Like other alcohol, wine helps some of us overcome our inhibitions, leading to unfettered and often exuberant personal expression … although hangovers and foggy memories do tend to compromise this creed somewhat.

The culture of wine is awash with the nuances of superior social status — hence the middle classes' love affair with fermented grape juice may go much further than is justified simply by its taste or effect. Since wine's discovery circa 5000 BC it has been drunk by those of high social status. The large amount of land and labour needed to make commercial quantities of wine has meant that this enterprise is usually the preserve of the social élite. Even when winemaking has been accessible to the masses (such as French and Italian peasants), rough wines have generally been their lot. Exquisite vintages have been reserved for the upper echelons; maintaining an impressive cellar requires time and energy. Wine has always provided élites with an activity that is aesthetically and intellectually stimulating.

You must be conversant with the unique aspects of grape varieties, the quality of distinct vintages, the *terroir* of different vineyards and similar subtleties.

The greater the personal experience of wine in Martinborough, from forming a bond with the winemaker to tasting whilst wandering among the vines, the greater the realisation of the individuated self. As Martinborough represents a site of rural authenticity — removed in time and space from the mundane lives of its visitors — tourists seeking the personal touch are on pilgrimages to their perfect selves. All pilgrimages, from the great religious movements to fans flocking to Elvis Presley's Graceland, involve a journey away from the petty, profane foibles of daily life towards a centre of perceived sacredness. This analysis then begins to explain why so many Martinborough tourists leave their dependants behind. The ideal individual is dynamic, spontaneous and a self-determining Romantic. Many of us choose to have children, but don't necessarily choose the children we have. Children can hamper

> *Tourists seeking the personal touch are on pilgrimages to their perfect selves.*

a parent's unfettered displays of individuality as changing nappies or providing taxi services to permanently disgruntled teenagers definitely eats into quality self-time.

But your lover may be an altogether different proposition. The presence of another free-willed adult who chooses to enjoy your exclusive company can be a robust and public endorsement of the self. Thus sharing a bath and an open fire with your darling in Martinborough can represent an attempt to experience authentic social intimacy (i.e. it's bloody nice) and correspondingly affirm yourself through the eyes, hands and private parts of another. Indeed, couples staying at one South Wairarapa homestay asserted these aspirations in the backyard gazebo so often that neighbours petitioned the owner to build a 2-metre fence around the property. Rural folk can only stomach so much pale, urban flesh entangled in the throes of natural passion.

For many wine buffs an audience with a renowned winemaker is akin to a Catholic receiving a blessing from the Pope

All pilgrimages also contain hardships that test the pilgrim's faith or readiness to receive divinity. The Rimutaka hill is a formidable geographical barrier that separates the capital city of Wellington from the blessed sites of Martinborough's vineyards. But other barriers — from having the financial means for a holiday to acquiring the cultural capital required to appreciate fine wine — must also be negotiated. The ease with which a person can transcend such barriers further marks their social status. Those who helicopter to Martinborough rank higher — and are thus more individually differentiated — than those massed together on bus tours. Likewise, wine buffs who regale dinner parties with stories of trips to the home of pinot noir in Burgundy or who refer to Martinborough winemakers on a first-name basis, are more distinctive than those who buy their pinot off the shelf at Woolworths.

Pilgrimage sites are also places where miracles are believed to have once happened and will happen again. In this respect Martinborough is one of the few places in the world noted for consistently producing top quality pinot — others being Burgundy, France and Oregon, USA. Many tourists, from wine novices to devotees, visit Martinborough to pay homage to the miracle of the grape. Personally meeting the winemaker is also a biggie. The winemaker is the high priest or priestess — a touchstone to the divinity of fine wine, a conduit between the mysteries of nature and the cultivation or culture of wine. For many wine buffs an audience with a renowned winemaker is akin to a Catholic receiving a blessing from the Pope. Not only does it recognise the celestial greatness of the winemaker but it also legitimates the connoisseur as a worthy follower, thereby enhancing the individuated sense of the self that many of us seek.

A pilgrimage is a quest to be redeemed or to reaffirm our faith. Martinborough's pinot pilgrims — like many tourists — seek to express their true selves through conspicuous displays of consumption, such as gourmet dining at the Martinborough Hotel or by sampling and buying Ata Rangi's expensive range of fine wines. Such acts conversely proclaim an individual's success in everyday — or rather workaday — existence. What's more, the tenets of individualism stipulate that a person should be able to make spontaneous, creative decisions — which is why tourists chide one another: "Go on, buy it. Treat yourself, you're on holiday!" When the weekend is over they return home reassured and revitalised, all the more secure and able to assert their sacred selves in daily life.

Historically, wine has been the tipple of the gods — from the frenzied Greek cults of Dionysus (later the Roman god Bacchus) through to its use in Christian communion. The world would have been bereft of many great champagnes if it wasn't for the viticultural teachings of the Benedictine monks in the Middle Ages. The spread of wine into the New World parallels the diffusion of Christianity to America, Australia and New Zealand. The first recorded planting of grapes in New Zealand was by the Anglican missionary Samuel Marsden at Kerikeri in 1819 to provide sacramental wine. He believed that if Maori could be taught the civilising pursuits of viticulture their conversion to Christianity would be more successful.

So pervasive is the quest for the free-willed, dynamic and successful self that many pundits believe that today's religion is that of the sacred self. This much-sought-after divinity of exalted individualism is clearly expressed through consuming illustrious commodities in public. Personal knowledge and experience of fine wine, the winemaker and the sacred site of its production can give an edge in the hotly contested identity and status games of the self-aware middle classes. In this light, Martinborough vineyards are monasteries of consumption to which the middle classes make pilgrimage and receive blessings that enhance their glorious sense of self. The jaded urbanites who tour Martinborough are not merely enjoying the pastoral delights of the New Zealand countryside, they are on retreat to their divine selves. *Salute* … and pass the loofah, my love!

Pop the corks of these vintage references:

Carrithers M (1985) *The Category of the Person: Anthropology, philosophy, history*, Cambridge University Press

Campbell C (1987) *The Romantic Ethic and the Spirit of Modern Consumerism*, New York, Basil Blackwell

Cooper M (1993) *The wines and vineyards of New Zealand*, Photography by Robin Morrison, Hodder & Stoughton
— (2002) *Wine Atlas of New Zealand*, Auckland, Hodder Moa Beckett

Douglas M (1989) *Constructive Drinking: Perspectives on Drink from Anthropology*, Cambridge University Press

Fuller R (1996) *Religion and Wine: A Cultural History of Wine Drinking in the USA*, University of Tennessee Press

Hall MC et al, eds (2000) 'Wine Tourism in New Zealand' in *Wine Tourism Around the World: Development, management and markets*, Oxford, Butterworth-Heinemann

Howland P (forthcoming) *Pinot Pilgrims: the production and consumption of wine, rurality and identity in Martinborough*, (Publishers queuing up. Honest!)

Johnson H (1998) *The Story of Wine*, London, Octopus Publishing Group Ltd

McCracken G (1990) *Culture and Consumption: New Approaches to the Symbolic Character of Consumer Goods and Activities*, Indianapolis, Indiana University Press

Robinson J (1995) *Jancis Robinson's Wine Course*, VHS video
— (1999) *The Oxford Companion to Wine*, Oxford University Press

X

"THE MIDDLE CLASSES ARE REVOLTING ... SERVE PINOT AT MY FUNERAL"

CLASS, POWER, REBELLION, WITCHCRAFT AND DEATH

ALL CULTURES AND societies are complex webs of power. The power of groups or individuals to dominate, command or influence others; to assert what meanings, values or moralities hold sway; to control what social roles, acts or relations individuals enjoy or endure — the clout to create lord and serf, owner and worker. Yet if all human existence orbits the axes of authority, then equally all domination is resisted. No power-holder, no matter how resourceful or malicious, can monitor all their underlings all the time, in every nook and cranny of their lives. In spite of your mother's warning not to spoil your appetite before dinner, did you not still scoff sweets on the way home from school? Meanwhile, the disaffected steal out in the dead of night to graffiti the walls of the powerful with words of protest. Even the brightest recesses of the mind — the realms of imaginative thought, play and desire — can remain hidden from the most efficient of tyrants. Under totalitarian regimes, where every thought and act is relentlessly bent to the will of dictators by compliant media, educators and state-supported bully-boys, many people can still envision their worlds upside down. Worlds where the meek inherit the earth, where white is black and black is white, or where motherhood is widely celebrated as a summit of human endeavour. Dominance is always resisted in stratified societies, such as ours, as individuals and groups inevitably have opposing interests which lead to conflict.

All cultures have assigned different social roles according to age and gender. However, once productive goodies are 'fenced' for the exclusive benefit of the owners, forms of unequal reward and social status start to emerge. Nomadic groups such as the !Kung San of the Kalahari Desert, who have little in the way of static food supplies, are for the most part egalitarian. Hunters and gatherers with access to permanent resources — such as the Kwakiutl of the American northwest and their salmon rivers — have robust pecking orders in all aspects of life. Stratification occurs whenever socially recognized differences — from kinship, marriage, 'race', religion, occupation and so on — are allocated unequal access to knowledge, political influence and material resources. It has been supported by a wide array of political systems ranging from the theocracies of ancient Egypt, the 'Big

Men' of Melanesia, Pacific chiefdoms, European feudalism, to our very own class-based, capitalist democracies. If individuals ever feel that such disparities are unfair, rebellion or resistance is likely. Conflict, however, does not always aim to overthrow the dominant — those at the top will fight each other for the spoils of the mighty, just as surely as those at the bottom will scrap over the crumbs. Hence we may have been equally fascinated with the squabbles between the late Princess Diana, Fergie and QEII for top-corgi status, and the traumatic showdowns between the white, black and sexually-wretched trash that fleetingly star on the Jerry Springer Show. But social inequality can also prompt co-operation, with shared interests banding together in lobby groups (Business Roundtable, Combined Trade Unions, etc) to combat those with divergent goals.

All resistance exists on a continuum between radical insurgence and conservative reform — between large-scale, open rebellion and small, everyday acts of hidden defiance. The latter include McDonald's workers who eat every 20th chip, tradesmen who do 'jobs' for each other and businessmen who operate two sets of accounting books. Anyone who openly rebels runs the risk of being detected and punished by those in power, whereas hidden resistance can undermine authority without being censured. Hidden resistance can be found in a variety of places, e.g. underground comics (*Jesus on a Stick*) and satirical websites (www.thekumara.com). The irony is that most resistance is actually directed towards maintaining the structures of inequality. Consider all the movements of change — e.g. the Luddites, the Russian/Cuban/Chinese revolutions, Mahatma Gandhi, the feminist movement. All have sought to change the way authority is expressed, especially by whom and how. None have resisted power in its entirety. The outcome has been to shift control away from current masters and into the hands of the mutinous. Individuals have rarely rebelled against inequality *per se*, but rather against their own drudgery. This is understandable; if power is inherent in all culture and society, then it is unavoidable. Better then to be powerful than powerless.

Yet the wielding of power does not necessarily result in an inequitable society. The Amish of Pennsylvania have distinct social roles, rights and responsibilities that are designated according to gender and age. Amish men control their farms, families, social politics and religion. The women sew, clean, cook and care for children. The roles are not open to negotiation. Although their positions in life may be unequal, the Amish see them as complementary and ordained by God. Even though clearly demarcated, the Amish nevertheless believe that all have equal status and value under the eyes of God. Meanwhile authentic communists everywhere hold fast to an ideal that although individuals may differ in talent, skill, intellect and beauty, this should not be rewarded by differences in political power, wealth and social rank. They dream of a day when cleaner, farmer, artist and neurosurgeon are equally valued and rewarded for their individual contributions to the social good.

The cultural and social worlds of New Zealand's middle classes are likewise riddled with the vicissitudes of power and resistance, though any opposition they display is usually conservative or reformatory. Have you ever heard a Kiwi crowd boo a lacklustre performance of the NZ Symphony Orchestra? They are more likely to applaud quietly, leave before any further ovation prompts another curtain-call and switch their allegiance to the NZ Chamber Orchestra. This moderate approach is partly due to their betwixt 'n' between status. Being neither at the bottom nor the top of the social ladder, they stand to equally lose or gain from any change to the status quo. Consequently they do not usually support the radical flattening or overthrow of established structures, no matter how inequitable they are. Such a move would compromise the advantage they currently enjoy over the white-trash bogans and ethnic minorities in the lower strata of our society. But neither do they vigorously support the status quo as this would deny them the opportunity to acquire the power, privilege and rank that is generally reserved for the top echelon of society — namely the assorted shareholding, CEO, landed and sporting nobility. The middle classes hedge their bets and agitate for better conditions and rewards within existing circumstances. On one hand they support New Zealand's class system, which enables some individuals by dint of hard work, skill and creativity to climb the ladders of prosperity. With the other hand they realise that such success is never guaranteed and that things beyond their control may stymie or derail an individual's progress. They also share an awareness that our economic and political systems are not perfect. Democratic capitalism can fairly be blamed for widespread environmental damage and social decline. There is little point in achieving prosperity only to find the water undrinkable and the streets beyond your walled subdivision besieged by crime. Hence the constant, steady-as-she-goes reformism directed towards building a better, brighter here and now. The middle classes are most likely to campaign for an improvement in line with their *existing* ideals rather than a total overhaul — for a clean, green environment; for higher standards of education and health; and for the ability — irrespective of gender, race or religion — to effectively express themselves in matters of employment, affairs of the heart or the marketplace.

As discussed in the introduction to this book, our middle-class existence can be seen as a never-ending quest for the authentic self — the self-determining and creative individuals we are taught to aspire to be. While our educational, financial and consumer experiences create a climate where our autonomy, choice and expression are considered paramount, everyday reality is altogether more restrictive and cruel. At work, home and in the supermarket many of us find that our ideals of the self-created person may be imaginary. Employment structures (e.g. 'glass ceilings' — invisible barriers to success) can halt the advance of even the most innovative and efficient person. All such systems attempt to focus our efforts towards a necessarily limited set of goals. Work is often repetitive, habitual and uncreative, reducing the unique person to just another cog in the mercantile wheel. Much of domestic life also exists beyond our control, reflecting poorly on our notions of the ideal, potent self.

Think about when your partner says no because s/he has a headache; when your dog drags your neighbour's rubbish across the front lawn; or when your teenage daughter pierces her nose or other body part, contrary to your express wishes. And there is little point in arguing with an eftpos machine that declines your card. The moral is that the middle classes' control over the minutiae of their existence is limited. So, in their search for a perfect world, where everyone can be true to their exalted sense of self, they are just as likely to argue with a waiter that their pinot noir be served at room temperature as they are to crusade for larger causes such as Greenpeace, dog control or against censorship of film festivals.

When individuals or groups rebel they react against but within existing structures of power; this appears to be true of most resistance. So when New Zealand's middle classes object to current arrangements — especially those that deny the creative and authentic expression of the self — they use knowledge, skills and technologies gleaned from these very same structures to frame their protests. Consider the following examples of middle-class resistance: the first is new-age religion, and more specifically feminist witchcraft, which only applies to a small subset of our society; the second, however, is common to us all — dying, death and (hopefully) remembrance.

Many Kiwis have a keen interest in new-age beliefs and practices. These can range from rubbing an auspicious crystal, taking a course of aromatherapy, joining a human potential movement such as yoga or transcendental meditation, to becoming a follower of neo-religious movement (NRM) such as new Pentecostalism, spiritual greenism, occult revivals and feminist witchcraft. The quest for a new religiosity is often a protest against our secular society and many new-age movements are crisis cults. NRM members often feel:

- Alienated from a meaningful social life
- Dissatisfied with scientific rationality
- Opposed to the established churches' exclusive claims to spiritual enlightenment
- Disillusioned with leftist politics
- That hierarchical establishments suppress their unique personalities.

In response, most NRMs are staunchly egalitarian, non-hierarchical and non-institutional. They maintain a holistic ethos in which all power — spiritual, intellectual, physical — is seen as universal, diffuse and accessible to all. They reject the dichotomy of mind and body, matter and spirit. NRMs make no exclusive claims to truth and celebrate a wide diversity of beliefs that individuals use to realise their total emotional, social and creative potentials. To NRMs the self is sacred; adherents seek salvation and paradise on Earth.

Two factors mark NRMs as unique in the history of crisis cults. The first is their emphasis on individualism in ideology and practice. The second is a membership that is almost entirely drawn from the ranks of the middle classes — especially the young, well-educated, well-travelled, relatively affluent and articulate members.

Individuals who subscribe to feminist witchcraft are a case in point. In Kathryn Rountree's words, the movement in New Zealand attracts women who are smart, arty, left-wing and right-brained. Like many other NRMs, feminist witches are encouraged to create a personal spirituality in response to their individual needs. A multitude of texts — from ethnographies of indigenous cultures to historical accounts of Nordic, Celtic and other pre-Enlightenment peoples — are trawled for philosophies, values and rituals. Believers weave these disparate elements together as the basis of their ever-changing, highly individualistic religious beliefs and customs. One feminist witch explained: "The Goddess is in me and in each of us and in everything … I pray to her a lot and meditate and she's like a friend to me or she's whatever I happen to be needing. It makes it very easy. I know she's not going to be anything other than exactly what I need." Whether divinity is seen as an overarching goddess, creative energy or the 'ultimate reality,' the individual believer creates a spirituality that makes sense to them.

Feminist witches do, however, share several beliefs. Foremost is that all spiritual powers and life forces — especially Goddess spirituality — are immanent and universal. The dictum of feminist witches throughout the world — *Thou art God/dess* — asserts personal sacredness and the universal sacredness of all others. Feminist witches also share two principles. One is the

Hence, the all-encompassing desire for personal growth and the rise in gym memberships, book clubs and dragon boat racing

Wiccan Rede: *And ye harm none, do as thou wilt.* Feminist witches may not harm others, but may invoke a self-protection spell. The other principle states that whatever we do will be returned threefold. Each witch may do whatever her ethics dictate, but these simple tenets effectively promote social responsibility and outlaw hexing.

Feminist witches clearly reject many of the structures that support the middle classes — from scientificism to patriarchy — although their emphasis on discovering and nurturing the authentic self directly appeals to a central middle-class ideal. Much of the knowledge, skills and values that we acquire through study, work, travel or daily consumer habits primes us to enter the realms of the creative mystic. Tertiary education, especially in the arts and humanities, promotes intellectual seekership and creativity, reinforcing in many of us the all-encompassing desire for continual personal growth. Hence the continual rise in gym memberships, book clubs and dragon boat racing. In addition, much middle-class employment (e.g. in bureaucracies, advertising, teaching) involves creatively manipulating symbols and meaning. Consider the worlds of books, advertising and movies — through which many of us are gainfully employed and many more are daily informed or entertained. In these realms Russell Crowe can just as easily be a Roman gladiator, schizophrenic egg-head or a half-wolf, half-cyborg and half-Aussie Rules player (I know the maths doesn't add up, but it's coming soon to a theatre near you!). TV docos and historical re-enactments also bring disparate peoples and distant times into our living rooms. These worlds of illusion and information provide a grab bag of symbols and ideas, thereby prompting individuals to create their own range of metaphors, meanings and messages themselves. The consumer ethic also promises that the authentic self will be realised through a never-ending array of improved shampoos, new season fashions and the latest in DVD players. So we spend most of our 'free-time' spending up large in a continual quest to creatively (and spontaneously) accessorise our lives. In comparison, NRMs resemble 'supermarket spirituality' in which middle-class mystics are encouraged to wander along the aisles of detached beliefs and practices, selecting those that most appeal and popping them into their egocentric, feel-good shopping baskets. One day it's Tantric sex, the next it is saying a quiet Celtic prayer to the god of the clean McDonald's toilet. And would you like self-actualisation with that order, sir/madam/gender-indeterminate?

When I discuss this topic women tell me they have no qualms being labelled feminist witches, but they baulk at the idea that they are middle-class, as this frames them within the social, economic and political structures they seek to resist and spiritually transcend. Yet these women are well-educated, well-travelled and hold down good jobs. The fruits of their lifestyle have clearly equipped them with the tools to embrace feminist witchcraft — as the sociologist Roy Wallis noted, "Affluence encourages idealism." Moreover, their resistance is allowed and compartmentalised by those in control. For all the power-brokers care, feminist witches could spend their entire weekends bathing in menstrual blood as long as they abide by the laws concerning the eating of little children, and turn up to work at 8.30 on Monday morning. In this sense NRMs are muffled forms of resistance that exist slightly off centre-stage, but with the stage manager's tacit consent. Should feminist witches disrupt the smooth flow of primary economic and political processes with their 'wacky' beliefs then watch out — all heaven will break loose and witchcraft trials will make a sensational return to the front pages of your daily newspaper.

While few of us know much about feminist witchcraft, most have had some experience of death. Dying, death and remembrance have been undergoing a change recently that can be directly attributed to the middle classes' desire to express their individuality. During the last century, dying in New Zealand became institutionalised as hospitals, funeral directors and churches cornered the mortality market. This contrasts dramatically with the period when most deaths occurred in the home. In New Zealand between 1867 and 1910 only 10% of people who died did so in public hospitals. You were far more likely to expire at home or work, surrounded by family, friends or workmates. The dead were laid out in their homes by a female relative or neighbourhood women versed in the art. Coffin making, funeral transport and even grave-digging were also voluntary, local affairs as friends and neighbours pitched in to ensure the departed were given a fitting send-off. With the rise of modern medicine and increasing numbers of hospitals, the ailing are now more likely to be away from home receiving treatment when they fall off the perch. In 1998, 65% of the 26,455 Kiwis who died did so in places such as hospitals or rest homes. Only 30% died at home and further 5% at work, on the road, at beaches or elsewhere.

An attitude change has accompanied this, especially among Pakeha. From being a normal aspect of life, death became something to be thwarted and repelled through the wonders of modern medicine. As death was problematised, sustaining life was equally affirmed as the

> *… the medical profession apparently draws no line between a hospital discharge by the front, side or back door*

ultimate ideal. For example, the Health Department measures the performance of hospitals in terms of the number of publicly-funded discharges (*Selected Morbidity Data for Publicly Funded Hospitals 1999/00*). A publicly-funded discharge may include release from hospital due to cure or it may simply refer to a patient's transfer to another medical facility for further treatment. Repeated treatments of a patient who returns with the same illness count as multiple discharges. And death — yes, death — during, or even because of, hospital care is likewise counted as a publicly-funded discharge. The medical profession apparently draws no line between a hospital discharge by the front, side or back door.

The advent of embalming is another case in point.

Embalming technologies have existed for centuries, but in the 20th century it became almost mandatory as the decomposing corpse drew attention to our ultimate failure to assert life over death, culture over nature. The dead were further set apart from the living by being kept in funeral parlours before burial — recent funerals in California have even been held with the cadaver completely absent from proceedings. There are few laws in New Zealand concerning the disposal of corpses. The Births, Deaths and Marriages Registration Act (1995) only stipulates that, once medical certificates and notices have been issued, bodies be "disposed of within reasonable time." The Burial and Cremation Act (1984), which regulates all burials, cremations and cemeteries except for Maori burial grounds, requires that individuals who die within 32km of a legally designated cemetery be buried or cremated there. Individuals may also be buried in recognised private burial grounds or in Maori burial grounds. You may be buried elsewhere as long as no District Court judge, local mayor or councillor objects that such action would be prejudicial to public health or decency. So your chances of being permanently planted under your favourite apple tree will depend on where you die, how liberal your local council is, or on the legal dexterity of your trustees. It is illegal to be cremated anywhere but a recognised crematorium, though interestingly the fine for an illegal pyre ($1000) is about the same as the cost of a legal one — which may encourage some to resist the status quo by lighting up in the backyard. Ashes can be spread anywhere, though where Maori or others collect food is likely to be seen as culturally offensive. Therefore it appears that among our middle classes — especially the Pakeha members — the typical funeral arrangements (i.e. the rituals of embalmment; viewing the deceased in a funeral parlour; adherence to standardised religious funerals, followed by burial or cremation) are as much a case of adhering to appropriate social customs as they are a matter of law.

All these structures and attitudes have been challenged recently as many of us have sought individualised dying, death and remembrance experiences. We believe that the institutions of death have denied both the dying and those grieving the freedom to fully express their personalities and sentiments. In a predominantly secular world, the religiosity of established churches and the quasi-religiosity of funeral parlours may appear archaic. Many of us have been to a funeral service where a priest delivered a stock eulogy that bore little relevance to the life of the departed. At my grandfather's funeral the officiating priest continually re-ferred to him as Francis, where anyone who knew him well would have called him Cam or Frank. Today, the middle classes — with their knowledge of the laws governing funerals, their encounters with the practices of other cultures (especially Maori), their relative affluence and heightened sense of self —

The fine for an illegal cremation is about the same as the cost of a legal one, which may encourage some to resist the status quo by lighting up in the backyard.

are seeking dying and funereal experiences that more properly reflect their unique personalities and they way they live(d).

Some plan their own funerals in detail — from choosing the music and ceremonies to be followed, to selecting the sites and types of burial. Ces Blazey, the widely-respected former chairman of the Rugby Union — and a man noted for his stellar capacity to plan ahead — organised his funeral eight years before his death. He asked an old friend to officiate at the service and carefully choose the hymns, including 'Guide Me, O Thou Great Jehovah' to reflect his great love of rugby and Cardiff Arms Park in Wales. Another prominent Kiwi decked out a station-wagon in the colours of his favourite rugby team and used this vehicle as his hearse — stopping at the rugby club for one last pint on the way to the church. Another literally 'sat in state' — resplendent in his white suit and safari hat — as mourners toasted him with pink gin and Arum lilies. Many now forsake church services altogether and call on the services of secular celebrants to oversee their final flings.

Others have built their own coffins in designs that reflect their lives, including ones carved with elaborate Maori motifs. One Rotorua woman has a business producing what she calls under-ground furniture. These are custom-made cabinets — some coffin-shape, other standard cupboard models — designed to reflect the personality of their owners. While alive you can use them as drink cabinets, wardrobes or linen cupboards. After death the cabinets revert to their functions as coffins. One man has a surfboard painted on his box, another is designing hers around a Swan Lake theme, while a third wants a plain cabinet so mourners can scribble farewell messages on the casket.

Even when it comes to the final resting place, many are choosing options that more eloquently express their sense of self. An Aucklander has already booked a 112m^2 burial plot in the Auckland Memorial Park to build a classic Roman-inspired crypt to house his final remains — and those of his Rolls Royce — at an estimated cost of $150,000. Another is planning to build a mausoleum with room for 80 people and complete with a kitchen (post-internment toasted sandwiches — now there's an afterthought). The more budget-conscious among us can buy a memorial planter, made from synthetic marble, in which the ashes are sealed below a decorative plant. The planter can be put in the deceased's favourite spot in the garden or even on the TV cabinet if you like. It can also be moved whenever its living descendants shift house, which can provide a great comfort to those left behind (and to those not left behind). With 70% of Kiwis choosing cremation, memorial planters are proving a hit.

All this is tame compared with how people in other countries have celebrated their own remembrance. The ashes of Malcolm Eccles of England are proudly encased in an egg-timer owned by his widow, Brenda: "I can't boil an egg to save my life. He knew that and said I should turn his ashes into an egg-timer." And Brenda thought she had laid that particular bone of contention to rest! When Barry Whittaker of Australia learnt he was dying from cancer, he began getting his body tattooed so that his skin could be preserved after death. "They're not just to last 20 or 30 years. They're to last generations of the Whittaker family," he said. A taxidermist removed his skin, resplendent with tattoos, before Barry was cremated and it is now displayed behind a bar at his son's place. In the US Mark Gruenwald, writer and editor of Marvel Comics, had his ashes combined with ink and then used to print the 12-part comic series Squadron Supreme as a single volume. His widow Catherine wrote in the foreword: "He has truly become one with the story and blended himself into the very fibre of the book." R.I.P — Rest in Print.

In New Zealand numerous 'home death' groups have been set up to assist their predominantly middle-class members to plan their final exit. Most of the members are female — an understandable bias as women generally outlive their male counterparts and our culture generally mandates that women be the guardians of social cohesion whatever the circumstances. Throughout the US and Europe there are supermarkets that offer a the full range of DIY funeral paraphernalia — including talking tombstones that literally allow the deceased to talk from beyond the grave.

Others have their last word by leaving pre-recorded electronic messages and visuals on www.finalthoughts.com which are sent to friends and relatives after their death. And let us not forget the rise of euthanasia societies who persistently demand the individual's right to choose to die, nor terminally ill patients who exercise their right to die at home.

Yet even within such apparently dramatic upheavals of dying, death and remembrance, resistance is mainly directed at middle-class expressions of the authentic self. Rest in self … or if you are a member of the New Zealand Cryogenics Society (www.igrin.co.nz/~nzcryosociety) — rest awhile, then be thy self … again. This particular rebellion seems liberating but still conforms to many of the structures that have long characterised death in New Zealand. Bodies are embalmed, buried or cremated; secular services generally follow patterns that reflect those of established religions: orations are given, tears flow and flowers are laid at gravesites, whether marked by trees or talking tombstones. No one is advocating eating the body of the deceased to honour their vitality of spirit, or the un-eulogy where those who are celebrating the demise of the deceased are given a chance to un-mercifully slate their memory. The power-brokers in the death industries have responded to this challenge by incorporating those aspects of resistance that pose the least threat and make the most profit. Many New Zealand funeral directors now adopt the attitude that as long as it's legal — and you can afford it — they'll do it. The established churches have been more circumspect, but don't be surprised to hear the tortuous strains of Led Zeppelin's *Stairway to Heaven* or the winter suite of Vivaldi's *Four Seasons* at the next religious funeral you attend.

Post-internment toasted sandwiches — now there's an afterthought

At my wife Karen's funeral we played some of her favourite Van Morrison songs and even Dave Brubeck's *Take Five* complete with drum solo. At Karen's request mourners were invited to take flowers from her casket, reflecting her love of gardening and her desire, even after death, to give to her friends.

While this discussion of NRMs and individualised death may be heavy duty, it's kind of fun to contemplate that whenever an individual fires up their BMW and jaunts over the Rimutaka hill to quaff Martinborough's fine wines and vineyards they are also rebelling. Only this time the resistance is directed against the constraints of daily life that thwart the unfettered expression of their ideal, fun-loving, total-consuming and ever-romantic selves (see the 'Pinot Pilgrims' essay, Chapter 9). It is also sobering to realise that this essay is yet another example of conservative resistance. Although I may rail against the resistance of the middle classes, I do so by using the educational, analytical and rhetorical tools that my particular middle-class existence has equipped me with. No banner-waving, bullet-dodging or dangerous espionage for me. I prefer to rattle cages with a glass of fine pinot noir in one hand and an art catalogue in the other. At the end of the day I am simply another neo-Marxist hedonist, who would like someone — anyone — to overthrow the material conditions of inequality so that I might enjoy the finer things of life without fear, favour or hard currency. Failing this — I'd quite like to win Lotto PowerBall!

Empower yourself with these references …

Aries P (1974) *Western attitudes toward death: from the Middle Ages to the present*, Baltimore, Johns Hopkins University Press

Baker E (1989) *New Religious Movements: A Practical Introduction*, London, HMSO Publications

Clark D (ed, 1993) *The Sociology of Death: theory, culture, practice*, Oxford, Blackwell

Cleave PW (1996) 'Dealing With Death: The Pakeha treatment of Death 1850-1910': unpublished MA in history, Wellington, Victoria University

Eilberg-Schwartz H (1989) 'Witches of the West: Neopaganism and Goddess Worship as Enlightenment Religions', *Journal of Feminist Studies in Religion,* (5) (1): 77-95

Foucault M (1980) *Power/knowledge: selected interviews and other writings*, translated by Colin Gordon, Sussex, Harvester Press

Neele KF (unpublished) 'Transitional Agency to the Grave and Beyond' Wellington, Victoria University

Rountree K (1993) 'Re-membering the Witch and the Goddess: feminist ritual-makers in New Zealand' PhD thesis, University of Waikato

Scott J (1990) *Domination and the arts of resistance: hidden transcripts*, New Haven, Yale University Press

Wallis R (1982) The New Religions as Social Indicators, in *New Religious Movements: a perspective for understanding Society*, New York, The Edwin Mellen Press

Westley F (1978) 'The Cult of Man: Durkheim's Predictions and New Religious Movements' *Sociological Analysis*, 39 (2): 135-145

Wolf E (1999) *Envisioning power: ideologies of dominance and crisis*, Berkeley, University of California Press

www.nzhis.govt.nz/publications/morb99-00text.pdf

XI

FITZGERALD'S PENIS IN A FICKLE WORLD

VALUE, QUANTIFICATION, NORMS & BODY WEIGHT

By ALL ACCOUNTS the American author F. Scott Fitzgerald was a natural talent — urbane, witty and socially astute. But Fitzgerald was also racked with angst and self-loathing. His creativity was often paralysed by criticisms of his writing and he obsessed about the smallness of his penis. So concerned was Fitzgerald with this subject that his equally famous peer Ernest Hemingway told him a truism that can be paraphrased as: *A man who looks down upon himself will always appear small.* Hemingway advised Fitzgerald that if he wanted a more positive outlook on life he should use a mirror instead.

Fitzgerald's misgivings evince a common cross-cultural belief that penis size and virility are linked. Cultures as diverse as the Dani of Irian Jaya with their large, ornamental penis sheaths and the physically impressive Shiva Linghams of India, all manifest varieties of the 'bigger is better' ethos. And as any adolescent Kiwi male who has experienced the after-rugby shower will know, one's place in the hierarchy of size is often asserted early in the season, usually by large — but not necessarily the largest — individuals. This ritual appraisal of club membership quickly creates 'us and them' cliques in the team, with the bigger boys asserting their superiority in all matters masculine, sexual and social — including soap and hot water allocation.

Hemingway's use-a-mirror advice to Fitzgerald combines a keen knowledge of optical foreshortening with an insight disputing that bigger is better. Hemingway hints that Fitzgerald's outlook was not only extremely limited, but it also reduced his sense of self-worth — to think less of oneself implies a negative comparison with the enhanced attributes of another and vice versa. Looking down upon either yourself or others reinforces a doctrine where all 'men' are neither created nor treated equally. If bigger really is better, then little is loathsome. In the eyes of many, a small-dick Fitzgerald simply would not have cut the mustard.

Most of us routinely use stereotypical measures to evaluate the worth of others we may only briefly encounter. This is partly due to the economic and social pressures of life today — we are highly transient, forever moving from idea to idea, job to job, place to place. Although highly generalised, stereotypes have a certain logic. For most of our daily lives we are surrounded by strangers, from bus drivers and shop assistants to the great unseen who eventually answer our 0800 phonecalls. This is especially true for urbanites, who account for more than 85% of us in New Zealand. In a world full of strangers, a fleeting glance may be all we get before we decide whether — or how — to pursue a more intimate social bond. As a result many stereotypical assessments tend to concentrate on the visual or aesthetic — to which different attributes are then ascribed: "He's only five foot five … he·must have short man's complex!" or "She's a DD at least. Must be a sexual goddess!" Such reasoning focuses on physical features that can be readily observed, easily described and reasonably guesstimated. The volume of a woman's ear lobe or the circumference of a man's wrist are usually missing from discussions that attach sexual/social value to different body parts. Yet when a character from the sitcom *Sex in the City* has a boyfriend with a 3-inch erect penis we can all cast knowing glances — he must be a descendant of Fitzgerald's!

While we may not always agree with stereotypes, we all use them to some extent. Think about how you would evaluate two men walking down an isolated dark street — one wearing Mongrel Mob patches, the other an Armani suit. Your response will be guided by your previous experiences with either 'type' of man. These can include personal experience — your cousin may be a patched gang member, your father a successful businessman. Conversely, your experience may be limited to the hype and stereotypes reinforced by the media. In which case you are likely to avoid the gang member and smile at the member of the Business Roundtable. Personally, I'd be wary of both.

But we are not simply socially mobile and transient, everyone from educators to marketers are constantly telling us that we are special, unique and capable of anything if well motivated. We — and indeed the whole damn world — are morally compelled to seek progress in whatever form: the promised land, the one great love, next week's Lotto draw, the next big idea … trouble is, this makes it all too easy to equate mere change of circumstances with progress (those in education, health and other sectors who are forced to endure frequent restructuring will start to froth and tremble about now). Amongst the middle classes there exists a sort of nervous restlessness that compels people to re-invent and change themselves in an endless search of a better life.

Even more nettlesome is that some have become so enamoured with change that shallow, essentially aesthetic and quantifiable measures can appear the only viable means of measuring one's upward mobility. A 20% increase in wealth, leg pressing 150 kilos in the gym, a lowered golf handicap, a cosmetically enhanced cup size — all become easily recognised markers of personal progress. When you're whizzing down the aisle of life on roller-skates organically embedded in your feet, you barely have time to judge a book by its cover, let alone stop and smell the roses. Even getting to know yourself is commonly done by external measures such as increased work productivity, CV updates and personal growth inventories.

The logic of quantification is remarkably seductive and comforting. It appeals to our Western-educated reason as abstract, ordered and predictable. Reduced to definite amounts, percentages and pie graphs, the infernal messiness of life — and especially such slippery, contestable and regularly indescribable qualities as worth, love, and success — are magically divorced from their grounded, cluttered realities and rendered manageable. The hope is that everything can be compared, assigned relative worth and then managed to our benefit. Fate, fickle gods, wild natural forces and the inevitable unpredictability of human life are thus tamed by the dictates of objectification. The truth of any situation is then expressed through means, modes and other equally malleable statistics. When you've got someone's — or something's — number, then you've got their reckoning in every sense of the word.

Indeed, the measures we are most likely to agree on are those of science (kilograms, centimetres, etc). These are seen as neutral in that they can be independently verified, calibrated and compared. Armed with a certified tape measure we could have agreed on the 'objective' length and girth of Fitzgerald's old fella. But while scientific measures may appear to surpass the stereotypical and subjective appraisals discussed above, they do not operate in social or cultural vacuums. The simple question of what is or isn't measured — let alone why and what necessarily follows — may alter over time as social concerns and the technologies of measurement change. Take body weight. At one level this measure is quantitative and objective. But when it

is transformed into ideas of what is a good or bad body weight, the scientific evaluation becomes loaded with qualitative or moral imperatives. Before the King of Tonga gave in to the imperialism of weight-loss, his immense size culturally signified his divine prosperity and the robust health of society. Nowadays the King is held up as an example of poor diet and bad health. When President Clinton put on a few pounds — or worse, indulged in intimate relations with a hefty intern — the moral outrage was heard around the world. Clinton partially redeemed himself displaying a deft sidestep and then jogging through the White House grounds, while Monica Lewinsky skipped along the golden path of Jenny Craig enlightenment.

Western medical concern about the links between our weight and health have combined with advances in science's ability to measure body-mass index (BMI), bone-density and body fat content, to work out whether we're of normal or abnormal weight. But normal for what? To lie inert on a couch and watch endless repeats of a perpetually dieting Oprah? To sit and read a never-ending stream of turgid, jargon-ridden academic articles? Or to be a fully productive and valued member of society? A medical diagnosis of correct or overweight is a moral measure, saturated with the dominant paradigms of economic, political and social life. The slogan *Healthy, wealthy and wise* neatly sums up the ideals of New Zealand and other Western societies today, which condemns the overweight to being *diseased, destitute and dumb*. Being fat and unproductive is rarely applauded as an act of rebellion against the social roboticism of today's keen, lean and mean corporate machines. On the contrary, eating to the point of obesity may represent a deep commitment to a pervasively consumerist society. Though doing a Mr Creosote — the exploding restaurant diner from Monty Python's *Meaning of Life* — probably misses the meaning of life in contemporary Western society where only sustained, long-life consumption enables an individual to take full stock of an ever-expanding, ever-changing commodity market. According to the productive and 'consumptive' ideals of the West, to die young is to die unfulfilled. Hence the rise of the Third Age — where such 'elderly' luminaries as Peter Snell exhort the over-60s to exercise regularly and eat healthily, so they may enjoy a rich and activity-filled life. Although frequent exercise and good diet won't necessarily boost your old-age pension to cover the cost of a month's hang-gliding in Bermuda, it will probably help you to mow the lawns and take out the rubbish with less difficulty. To truly enjoy your dotage you will also need a well-fed super-annuation scheme.

Scientific techniques of quantification were highly sophisticated in Europe by the 15th century. This pivotal moment in history was also the beginning of the colonial quest for exotic peoples and places. European imperialism led to the vast expansion of global trade and foreshadowed a growing commitment to the dictates of the market economy. Basically, a market economy decrees that anything can be commodified and exchanged for profit, and that this can take place between anybody, whether friend or foreigner. In a market economy most trade occurs between strangers — euphemistically termed clients, customers or retailers. Under these circumstances no history of trust or fair trading necessarily exists between them. The potential for deceit is obvious as opposing parties seek to maximise gain and avoid loss. Rampant profiteering, shoplifting, fixed cricket matches and used-car salesmen are all predictable outcomes of a market economy and trade between strangers.

The sciences of quantification are vital in giving universal criteria of exchange that parties can use to check out the fairness of any trade. A box of apples is an ambiguous commodity and open to myriad personal interpretations. Is the box half empty or half full? In contrast, a kilo of apples is a definite amount, able to be measured, verified and agreed on. The juiciness of the apples is still anyone's guess, although ENZA — the agency that exports our apples and pears — dedicates enormous resources to refining measures of quality, from the starch pattern index (SPI) readings to penetrometer measures of flesh-firmness. Nevertheless the value of an apple still exists somewhere between the depth of the buyer's desire and wallet, and the size of the seller's overdraft.

As a general dictum, the more negative the trade — i.e. the more one party benefits at the expense of another — the weaker the social bond. Conversely, the more generalised the exchange where no parties keep accounts, the more intimate and potentially enduring the involvement. Exchange between close family members is in the nature of gift giving and is not usually subject to the same scientific measuring or commercial accounting regimes as commodity trade in a market economy. With the increasing use of 'market logic' to define a whole raft of social and cultural phenomena — from the provision of health services to the worth of academic research — it is not hard to imagine a time when all domestic work and other labours of love will be dispensed at current market rates. Family members will present each other with monthly invoices: lawnmowing after school $30; $1000 for every hour of labour before 6cm dilatation, an increase of 20% for every hour thereafter … and so forth.

Our faith in science is not limited to its ability to quantify and enable exchanges between strangers. We also believe it can record, predict and overcome 'nature.' This belief also emerged in 15th century Europe and later formed the basis of the Enlightenment. Science's 'quantitative feel for nature,' which culminated in 20th century probability mathematics, aimed to reveal the normalcy that underpin the seeming chaos of nature, 'man' and society through the use of statistics. Thus we now believe that once 'natural laws' are known, we can predict and control our futures. Testing for genetic tendency towards cancer, and undertaking proactive treatment (e.g. radical mastectomies) before any actual sign of illness, is one example of this ethos. Rather than believing that our lives are subject to fate or chance, we now observe and statistically analyse all known variables so that we can actively manipulate them to ensure a favourable outcome. Risk-taking — once a leap into the unknown — has become a valued and rational enterprise. Hence the meteoric rise of corporate 'risk managers,' contract lawyers and human resource departments.

Rampant profiteering, shoplifting, fixed cricket matches and used-car salesmen are all logical outcomes of a market economy and trade between strangers

But quantification, risk assessment and control tend to focus on criteria which are easily calculated, and not on other variables (e.g. values, expectations) which may be as influential, but prove more elusive to robust measurement. The world-renowned biologist Stephen J. Gould, on being diagnosed with incurable abdominal mesothelioma, was told that this deadly cancer had a median mortality of about eight months. To most people this would suggest that he would likely be dead in eight months. But medians are merely abstractions worked out from the complete range of known experience. At one level our lives are marked by incredible variety. When Gould investigated where he was on the range for his type of cancer, taking into account his socioeconomic status, self-described positive attitude and other lifestyle factors, he found he was in the right-skewed group of individuals who could reasonably expect to live many years beyond the median point. In fact Stephen J. Gould did not yield until 2002 — nearly 20 years after he was first diagnosed. As Gould stated, for him the "message was not in the median."

My most vivid encounter with the normalising tendencies of science was when my son Estlin was born prematurely. It was a dark and stormy night … the Rimutaka hill road was closed by snow and Masterton Hospital was not well equipped to handle a six-week prem. According to the attendant experts — midwives, nurses, obstetricians and paediatricians — Estlin's early arrival meant that he could potentially suffer from a range of problems. Yet as a child cannot be born any earlier than when it is delivered, I wondered: "Six weeks earlier than what?" Estlin's premature status was decided through a comparison with the average length of all previously recorded human gestations. This revealed that Estlin's birth was later than some, earlier than others. Once again, to work out normalcy the statistical focus was on the averages, medians and modes — not on the total range.

So if variation is the norm, why was Estlin's 'early birth' a problem? Experience had taught the experts that children born six or more weeks earlier than a period of 40 weeks may be physically and intellectually disadvantaged compared to most children who go full term. But what — and who — determines advantage or disadvantage? We are all born with and acquire a whole range of different capabilities over our lifetimes — be these short or long. Once again variation is the norm. A healthy infant is pretty much defined as one that will eventually grow and fully embrace adulthood — which could cynically mean one who fulfils its destiny to be a robust producer and consumer of global capitalism. Although definitions of early, late or ideal births may be backed up by the weight of sound medical knowledge, they are still moral constructs. As it happened, the placenta on which Estlin was reliant had degenerated and the umbilical cord had wrapped around his neck four times. If live birth was the goal, then Estlin's arrival was not a moment too soon.

After he had arrived safely — i.e. without any culturally determined complications — he was soon prey to the next battery of normalcy tests from the kind and supportive Plunket nurses who visited weekly. They graphed his weight, height, even the size of his head (it's possible they even measured the length of his new fella). Estlin's results were compared with a standardised range derived from other tiny tots to plot his physical and mental growth. The Plunket nurse would announce whether Estlin was below, above, or normal for his age. If the result was below par then mitigating circumstances — such as his prem birth — were factored in and their possible influences analysed. A variety of remedies, from feeding Estlin more often, to stimulating him with coloured cards hanging above his cot, would be recommended. Although it was obvious that the Plunket nurses were acting in what they thought were the best interests of the child, there was no acknowledgment of the particular social, cultural, political and economic influences that had created these 'interests'.

While I may appear to be critical of medical science, I am happy to report that Estlin has grown to be a decidedly healthy, intelligent and thoroughly 'normal' boy. At the time around his birth I felt uneasy with the normalcy tests and interventions he was subjected to. It seemed that the social die was being cast far too early and within extremely narrow parameters. I remember thinking as I held that little bundle in my arms — there, but for the grace of being born slightly above-average, go I.

If parents choose, Plunket-type measuring and evaluation can continue until a child is of school age. Once deemed to be within an acceptable range of physical and mental development, the child is then most likely to be exposed to a different series of normalcy tests — ones that last for the next 10 to 12 years — i.e. going to school. Schooling is where our progress — in learning how to read, write, do sums, use computers, time-keep, engage in 'appropriate' social behaviour and so on — is subject to regular monitoring and modification according to various educational and social norms. One of the main reasons for state-controlled education is to gauge our relative competencies with the express aim of directing us towards divergent adult pathways. Those deemed average or above average may be herded towards tertiary study and professional careers, while those thought to be inferior are directed towards toilet and street cleaning — though little in our schooling will have directly equipped us for such work.

Even as fully-fledged adults the normalcy testing and social-economic disciplines do not end. How well we work is subjected to efficiency reviews and peer comparison, while Inland Revenue officials, Commerce Commissions and an array of other bureaucracies constantly evaluate our performance to ensure we act — and are being treated — appropriately, according to an onslaught of fiscal, contractual, legislative and social standards. From womb to tomb our lives are prone to constant testing and correlated social discipline. Step outside the norms that regulate our existence — fart in public, shout at the moon, wear a bala-clava in a bank — and you are likely to attract swift censure to bring you back into line. And if this is not possible, steps are taken to ensure the continued legitimacy of the norms, usually by placing errant individuals firmly outside the normal — e.g. in jail, psychiatric units or simply beyond the pale.

If you don't believe me try this simple test next time a shopkeeper engages you in typical chit-chat and asks if you've had a busy day. Respond with a look of incredulity and reply: "God no, I never work hard! I try to avoid work altogether. Benefit fraud is the life for me." At a minimum this should ensure you are served briskly and without fanfare in the future.

Had F. Scott Fitzgerald lived longer, he would have witnessed an explosion in the 'science' of penis augmentation and might have been moved to subject himself to a litany of pills, potions and pulleys. A host of urologists, sexologists and questionable others now employ a variety of 'scientific' techniques — from laser surgery, silicon injections, milking exercises, vacuum pumps, and complicated weight systems — in attempts to lengthen and enlarge penises. Given that the recorded range of erect penises varies from less than 1, to more than 13 inches, there may be scope for movement one way or another. But whether the scientific development of larger penises is possible perhaps misses the point. Firstly, penises come in a hotchpotch of shapes, sizes and lengths. If every man were able to enlarge his dimensions by the same degree, then the same range of sizes would be maintained. Of course, this scenario assumes an ideal world where all men have equal desire, access and financial wherewithal to avail themselves of such resources. However, like penises, these are not equally distributed in the real world. So even if the science of enlargement is credible, only those suitably desperate and with large wads of cash will be able to truly claim they are the biggest dicks in town.

Of course, whether large or small is better is fiercely contested. There are a swag of narratives — from sex magazines to '9 inch clubs' — which stoutly proclaim that bigger is better. But there is also research that shows many people simply don't care, find large schlongs physically uncomfortable in one way or another, or who rate personality and other factors as more important. Large or small, important or trivial, we will draw on these narratives and on our own experience to make up our minds. For some, every centimetre will be a godsend, while others won't even bother to look. Personally, I have always preferred the writing of William Faulkner.

Some large and some lesser references:

Crosby AW (1997) *The Measure of Reality: Quantification and Western Society, 1200–1600*, Cambridge University Press

Douglas M (1992) *Risk and blame: essays in cultural theory*, London, Routledge

Foucault M (1970) *The order of things: an archaeology of the human sciences*, London, Tavistock

Gould SJ (1985) 'The median isn't the message' *Discover*, 6: 40-43 Also at http://cancerguide.org/median_not_msg.html

Hacking, I (1990) *The taming of chance*, Cambridge University Press

Lindenbaum S & M Lock (eds, 1993) *Knowledge, power and practice: the anthropology of medicine and everyday life*, Berkeley, University of California Press

Lock M (1998) 'Breast Cancer: Reading the Omens' *Anthropology Today*, 14(4): 7-16

Meyers J (1985) *Hemingway: A Biography*, New York, Harper & Row

www.the-penis.com Web-site dedicated to "male sexuality, male sexual health, masculinity, and the joy of being a man"

INDEX